Praise for *Findir*

"Having a family like Theo's redefine
about physical, spiritual, and emotional
When there is love, anything is possible, and *Finding Theo* is a testament to exactly that. This story is extraordinary and will encourage its readers to be courageous in their own lives!"

—Alana Nichols, 3x Gold Medalist, US Paralympic Team
First Female American to Win Gold in both
the Summer and Winter Games

"*Finding Theo* invites readers inside a father's perspective of a family's desperate struggle to remain balanced against the determination and independent spirit of their critically injured son who rejects the prognosis about his future. It is an extraordinary story of strength, courage, and faith."

—John Donovan, Chief Executive
Officer, AT&T Communications

"Some patients need a gentle nudge to move forward while others, like Theo, are disciplined and focused on day one. *Finding Theo* is the story of how this brave young man, his dedicated family, and his determined care team banded together to achieve his remarkable outcomes."

—Craig Hospital Foundation, Englewood, Colorado

"It was an honor and a privilege to have been a part of Theo's miraculous journey. His determination, strength, and spirit were inspiring to me and all who encountered him throughout. *Finding Theo* is a testament to the capacity of the human spirit."

—Dr. Kirk D. Clifford, MD, Rocky
Mountain Orthopedic Associates

"*Finding Theo* reminds us of what is good and important. Theo, together with his family and the many heroes who were part of his journey, are shining examples of the strength of the human spirit. Their courageous story is an inspiring reminder that, even faced with what appears to be an insurmountable challenge, *giving up* is not an option."

—Jim Falk, President & CEO, World Affairs Council of Dallas/Fort Worth

Finding Theo

Timothy Krause

Clovercroft Publishing

Finding Theo

©2018 by Timothy Krause

Published by Clovercroft Publishing, Franklin, Tennessee

Published in association with Larry Carpenter of Christian Book Services, LLC www.christianbookservices.com

Lyrics from "Traveling Mercies" by Billy Crockett and Milton Brasher-Cunningham used by permission

Gregory Orr, excerpt from "Not to make loss beautiful" from *Concerning the Book That Is The Body of The Beloved*. Copyright © 2005 by Gregory Orr. Reprinted with the permission of The Permissions Company, Inc., on behalf of Copper Canyon Press, www.coppercanyonpress.org

Edited by Lee Titus Elliott

Cover Design by Suzanne Lawing

Cover Illustration by Kim Stanley Bonar

Interior Layout Design by Adept Content Solutions

Printed in the United States of America

ISBN: Hardcover   978-1-948484-13-8
        Trade Paperback   978-1-945507-92-2

"The farmer stands at the fountain head—he is closest to the source. He knows for sure, 'God sendeth the rain.'"

—Lewis Krause, Scattered Abroad

Contents

For Jorja, Theo, and Mae

Foreword

George A. Mason

"The world breaks everyone," Hemingway wrote, "and afterward many are strong in the broken places." If we live long enough, we will find this empirically true. None of us gets out of this life unscathed, so it's not the scathing but how we respond to it that defines us.

Finding Theo is one father's story of his son's courageous battle for life and a return to "normal" and how that struggle forces the father to explore his own understanding of miracles, faith, and coincidence. It probes the question of whether there are universal forces at work in the world in mysterious and wondrous ways.

Theo Krause grew up under my watchful eye. He and his family are members of the church family I serve as pastor. They are part of a congregation of seekers who share their own journeys to "find Theo" and discover strength in coping with the broken places.

Whether you believe in God, practice a faith, or only wonder about mysteries that beg rational explanations, in *Finding Theo,* you will discover a reason to keep searching. This is no simple account of tragedy to triumph, no mere inspirational tale that will move you to try a little harder. At every turn, this book will invite you to confront the limits of what you think you know and what you think you have in you to believe. Then it will ask you what you want to do next.

Someone has said that faith is walking to the edge of all the light you have and taking one more step. When a father's son is critically injured, that step can lead to a chasm. Faith becomes a way of looking at the world with more trust than cynicism, believing that underneath the seeming randomness of events there lurks a conspiracy of goodness and kindness. Chaos gives way to order, woundedness to wellness, and despair to hope.

Some believe there's an invisible divine hand guiding all things. If that's true, it's likely God's off hand—the weaker hand of love that comforts us and cheers us on, rather than the dominant hand that directs and steers. It's a hand that gives us a hand, rather than taking ours away. This partnership of seen and unseen powers requires patience and respect, a mutuality that can only be known by time and pain.

There's a Japanese craft called *kintsukuroi* that translates "to repair with gold." It's the art of repairing pottery with gold or silver lacquer and understanding that the piece is all the more beautiful for having been broken *and* repaired in this costly way. By means of *kintsukuroi*, the vessel continues to show where it was broken, but now the very scars that reveal its damage show up as the most valuable part of it.

A father frustrated while standing by and watching his son suffer discovers a depth of resilience and courage in his child he could not previously fathom. His son's refusal to give up, the capacity for pushing himself beyond what his medical team and parents can imagine, and his insistence that he will return to his former self illustrate the strength of repairing "broken places." Is his recovery a miracle? Does the miracle help our believing more than our believing makes the miracle? Are miracles more likely unanticipated breakthroughs in nature than the suspension of nature? Now and then, a confederacy of good will pushes through the slow processes of nature's fall and rise, speeding the renewal to the point we can view it with awe.

The spiritual life teaches us how to live well through suffering and brokenness. It points us to the place where wholeness and wellness are found. Once in a while, we are privileged to see how spirit conquers flesh without the need to conjure or cajole. It just makes itself at home in a heart and calls a body to order.

Theo's good father, Tim, is my good friend. *Finding Theo* isn't meant to be his story, but it is, as the story of any son is the father's story as well. Because we share one humanity, this book is also my story of "finding Theo." I suspect it will be your story, too.

Hemingway didn't venture into religion per se when talking about getting stronger in the broken places, and neither does Tim Krause. The search for meaning may be the essence of religion, but sometimes religion itself gets in the way of that search. A story, on the other hand, especially a true human drama like *Finding Theo,* invites you to do that work yourself along the way. With luck or grace (who knows which or why?), you may find yourself stronger in the broken places.

Rev. George A. Mason, PhD
Senior Pastor
Wilshire Baptist Church
Dallas, Texas

1

Finding Theo

Four young men on mountain bikes pause at a scenic overlook to catch their breath. The crisp fall air stings their lungs as they gasp for sparse oxygen. The high afternoon sun filters through the aspens, and beads of sweat trickle down their flushed cheeks. Their grueling climb to the top will be rewarded with the exhilaration of the downhill ride they have been anticipating all day.

One rider speeds ahead of the pack and stops to video the others as they whiz by, laughing, then repacks his camera and jumps on his bike to catch up. The earthy smells of the forest floor fill his nostrils as he gains speed, descending into a deep ravine. He spots a pair of humps in the single rutted path and, in a split-second, decides to jump them. The trail takes an awkward turn just past his landing. He launches through the air, violently striking the base of a lone aspen tree headfirst.

He awakens, splayed on the ground facedown, when another lone mountain biker stops and asks, "Hey, man. Are you okay?"

The injured rider's face is tight with pain. He mutters that he is having difficulty getting up and just needs a little help. Soon two women arrive on the trail, push their bikes aside, and stoop to help him up, but they instantly realize his hands are limp and he has almost no strength in his arms. Two more women bikers appear, and they help remove the young man's backpack and ease him onto his back. One of the women unlatches his chin strap, gingerly removes the helmet, and tosses it aside without a glance. They know they need to call for help, but they are twenty miles from the nearest town, ten thousand feet up in the mountains, and at least two miles from the bottom of the trail. There is no cell service.

The lone rider who was first to find the young man knows what to do next: go for help up the mountain. He jumps across the small brook running alongside the trail and disappears up the steep mountain terrain, scrambling on all fours. He picks his way up the slope, running on pure adrenaline, frantically dialing 911 on his cell phone as he goes.

"Nine-one-one. What is your emergency?" he hears as his cell phone finally connects. Breathlessly he blurts out what he has seen and gives precise directions about where the injured rider is on the trail. He reports that the fallen rider cannot feel his extremities. The operator instructs him to do everything possible to keep the young man warm and emphasizes that it is impossible to guarantee exactly how soon a rescue team can arrive.

Meanwhile, the four women have turned their full attention to the injured rider. Two of them spring into action as if by instinct. Their first priority is to keep him warm and awake to prevent him from going into shock, or worse, from falling into a coma if he has a concussion. One of the women rips through her backpack to retrieve the survival blanket she always carries just in case of an emergency but has never had to use until now. She cocoons him in the blanket, carefully tucking it under his sides, to keep him warm. Together, the two take up posts sitting cross-legged on opposite sides of the rider and massage his hands and feet to keep the circulation moving.

The other two women decide to start down the trail to find more help. As they descend the winding path through a clearing, they pass the injured rider's three companions, who are backtracking. The three men soon find their injured friend sprawled under a tree between the two women who remained behind and are working to keep him comfortable as he drifts in and out of consciousness.

A rescue operation, triggered by the 9-1-1 call, is beginning to take shape. A Care Flite rescue team is on standby but still sixty miles away. A specialized wilderness search-and-rescue team, still bleary from a flood-rescue operation the day before, is assembling at their headquarters. Within an hour, they have converted the dirt parking lot just above a river at the entrance to the trail into an emergency-rescue base teeming with people, vehicles, and equipment, and a helicopter is in the air. Now, time is what matters most.

At the accident site, the lengthening afternoon shadows begin to cast a fall chill over the group, and clouds gather over the ridge, threatening a thunderstorm. Ignoring their own discomfort in the chilly evening breeze, they all pile their jackets across the young man's shivering body as it fights to protect itself against the shock and the pain.

The two women pepper him with questions and occupy him with conversation not only to keep him from falling asleep but also just to keep his mind off his predicament. The young biker cannot feel his chest and, having no sensation of his own breathing, senses he is drowning. As time drags, he desperately needs to shift his weight. His rear is numb, and he aches with pain in his back and neck. He cannot move his arms or legs, and the women resist his pleas to help him reposition himself, afraid to injure him more.

The biker forces himself to remain calm. In the quiet, he stares at the sky and thinks, "This is where I will die." The undulating trees open to a patch of blue sky, where puffy white clouds meander through the frame. It draws him in like a glowing campfire or a mysterious window to an unfamiliar world. It is his idea of what heaven must look like.

The women can see when his thoughts drift and his eyes fill with fear. "Pain in my back . . . can't feel my hands and feet . . . won't walk again." One gently cradles his head with her warm hands, saying with all the certainty she can muster, "Don't worry. Just be still. They will come and take care of you." The light touch of her fingers stroking his hair reminds him of his mother's touch, and it calms him. "Why are you here . . . now . . . doing this?" he wants to know.

At the makeshift emergency-rescue base, an anxious mission commander listens for news from the first team of rescuers now scrambling up the trail. A second team, responsible for the logistical and technical aspects of the hike, caches rope and other climbing equipment at strategic points along the trail in case a helicopter exit becomes impossible.

Past the most difficult part of the trail, lugging heavy equipment through steep switchbacks and around massive boulders, the first rescue group picks up its pace. They cross an open ridgeline, drop into a crease, and begin a steady climb into a long gulch as the foothills steepen on either side. The trail is well defined, a single smooth dirt rut cut a half a foot into the forest topsoil and just wide enough to walk, with shin-high grass growing on either side. Three miles in, they round a bend and finally catch sight of three mountain biking friends huddled above two women who are sitting on either side of the injured biker.

The welcome sight of the rescue team coming up the trail unleashes an almost euphoric sense of relief among the young man's caretakers. Waiting gives way to action. The biker's friends step back and watch the pros take over, working with practiced precision to triage their patient and stabilize him.

They hear the helicopter hovering in the distance, but the lead paramedic on the ground already knows that reaching the helicopter poses a problem. He has been communicating with his colleague on board, and the pilot has burned off enough fuel to accommodate the weight of his additional passenger, but the team on the ground cannot find a landing spot. They agree the pilot should search for a clearing while the rescue team starts down the trail.

The pilot crisscrosses the gulch, looking for a landing, and the onboard paramedic scans the forest for a sign of the rescue team and catches a glimpse just as the team passes through a small clearing about a half-mile down from the accident site. The pilot spots the open top of a rock abutment on a ridge parallel to the clearing, a tight space about the size of a two-car garage against a hundred-foot bluff on one side, with a sea of fallen pine trees scattered around the other side like the start of a big game of pick-up sticks. Not quite level, the rock surface slants toward the cliff edge, but it will have to do.

The rescuers veer from the trail and begin picking their way, hoisting their patient gingerly along in the litter, more than a half of a mile up the steep embankment toward the bluff. Navigating over and between the fallen trees, stumps, and boulders and through the soft, loose footing, one rescuer steers the litter, two more steady the sides, and two more walk ahead, calling out rocks and holes to avoid, keeping their patient as stable as possible. Others clear the path, haul gear, or position themselves nearby to take over for a tired colleague.

The pilot maneuvers the helicopter down on the rock, hoping it is level enough and big enough to accommodate the landing skids and accessible enough for the rescue team to get to him. He drops in for the landing. The onboard paramedic slides the cargo door open to survey the surroundings in the last few feet before the helicopter touches down. He glances back at the tail rotor and shouts a warning to the pilot just seconds before the rotor can strike a protruding stump. The pilot corrects just in time to avoid a crash and repositions the helicopter to a solid landing. They wait, with the rotors still turning to provide a beacon of sound for the team on the ground. The paramedic jumps out to hike down around the bluff and help bring the injured biker to the helicopter.

Main rotor blades spin to a deafening roar. As the helicopter lifts off, the lead paramedic looks down at the young man lying on the deck beneath him, the patient's head braced just between his feet. To the flight crew, the young patient seems calm, but the paramedic can imagine what lies ahead. They all know this young biker is in trouble. His name is Theo. He is my son.

2

The Call in the Night

T he helicopter disappears into the night as an intense lightning show rips across the western sky. The flight is solemn, except for the steady, ominous drone of the helicopter blades cutting the air. Somewhere below, three impatient friends are hurtling down the highway to find Theo at the hospital. The beautiful mountain scenery retreats beyond the reach of their headlights. In one car, Dan Miller stares out the passenger window as Eric Sjoreen concentrates on navigating the road ahead. Only the sound of the engine straining against an uncertain, winding road and the bikes rattling against each other in the back of the jeep break the eerie silence. Scott Everhart is driving Theo's car, where a cracked helmet rolls around in the back seat, giving in to every curve.

Fewer than twenty-four hours have passed since the group of friends stopped their cars at the top of McClure Pass on the way to Crested Butte to admire the spectacular sunset and to consider how fortunate they were to be living in such a beautiful place. Long gone, now, is the flush of anticipation on their faces. Plans have changed, and Dan must find the words to tell Theo's parents about what has happened. Dan is Theo's friend and also his work supervisor. Dan invited Theo on the trip and feels responsible.

He stares down at his cell phone and slowly punches in a number. I am sitting on the couch and watching TV when the house phone rings. Only solicitors, the alarm company, and my wife's relatives ever call that number, so I let it go to voice mail. When no one answers, Dan tries a second number, my wife's cell phone.

When Jorja answers, Dan introduces himself as one of the friends with whom Theo had gone riding in Crested Butte. In a quiet tone, he finally breaks the news.

Jorja grabs a notepad brightly decorated with a green-and-blue floral design. She scribbles as Dan speaks:

> *Hurt neck -*
> *flew*
> *him to Hosp*
>   *St. Mary's*
>   *Grand Junction*
> *Concussion?*
> *Couldn't/didn't move feet @*
>   *1st —now better.*

The next thing I hear is a terse "Tim, come here now! Ted is hurt!"

I scramble off the couch and stand in front of her, listening to one side of the conversation as Dan tells her as much as he knows. Jorja wants to know more. He does not have more but will call again when he does. In the instant it takes to hear the simple "click" of a disconnected call, time hangs for us.

Jorja and I stare at each other. We have no clue what to do next. Do we wait? Do we call someone? Do we book plane tickets? My heart is pounding so hard it makes my shirt flutter with every beat. I feel as if I am jet lagged, out of breath from a hard sprint, and sick to my stomach from eating too much pizza.

We rationalize the news might be better than it sounds, maybe just a concussion and a couple of broken bones. Still, Jorja calls Theo's younger sister, Mae, who is home from college but out with friends. She turns to a friend and says, "It's my brother. I wonder what he's done this time." The tone in her mother's voice is serious, so she decides to come home. We wait for hours. No news. For hours.

Jorja and I sit on the floor in my study and cry as night caves in on us.

Time is scarce, however, in Grand Junction at St. Mary's Hospital. It is a short trip from the helipad down the elevator chute and directly into the emergency room on the main floor. Technicians, nurses, and doctors swarm. A scan is ordered, and Theo is whisked off to radiology. The on-call surgeon waits impatiently for the images to be processed. As the pictures tile across the computer screen, he winces. Theo's neck looks like a derailed train. Joints are jammed together, and the vertebrae are twisted, pinching, but not breaking, the spinal artery. A shard of bone appears embedded in Theo's spinal cord wall.

The surgeon scans the emergency room schedule. An operating room is open and ready. Coincidentally, his best spinal-surgery team is also on call tonight. His orders set off a flurry of activity. Oblivious to the way conversations pause and hospital staffers steal glances as he and the attending physician pass by in the hallway, he discusses the complexity of the repair procedure with her and what they are about to tell their patient.

Pushing through the doors into the quiet but brightly lit pre-op room, they find Theo behind a half-closed curtain. A white blanket, fresh from the oven, is neatly draped across his hospital gown. An IV drip port is installed in his left hand, and a bundle of wires monitoring his vitals converge on a set of machines keeping sentinel near the headboard. His cycling clothes have been cut off his body and are in a plastic bag stuffed under the bed. The two doctors pull the curtain closed behind them. No family is there to hold Theo's hand or keep him company. His friends are still a half-hour away.

The surgeon glances at the monitors to check vitals and flips through the chart. Theo's low pulse rate sets off the monitor alarm, and the nurse reaches up to silence it. "I'm in pretty good shape right now," Theo explains. "I'm road biking a lot, and I'm lifting weights, getting myself ready for the snowboarding season. So something in the forties is normal for me." After a brief introductory conversation, the surgeon knows he is dealing with a no-nonsense personality. He gets right to the point. "You have broken your neck. Realistically, you are not going to walk again, but we are going to do our best to make it so that you can get use out of your arms."

Theo takes the news with a steely glare of defiance as the doctor delivers his prognosis. Theo nods his head in understanding, though, and sets his jaw tight to fight back tears. The doctor explains the procedure, asks if there are questions, and slips out to finalize his preparations for the surgery. The attending physician stays behind to keep Theo company. They decide it is time to call home with an update.

Our house phone rings again at 2:00 a.m. This time, I answer immediately, and Jorja picks up the extension. "Mr. Krause, this is Gina Martin. I'm the attending physician in the ER tonight, and I'm here with your son." Her tone is measured and clinical but friendly. As she talks, her confident, calming manner says, "Don't worry. We know what to do. He is in good hands." She tells us what the triage revealed. He has broken two vertebrae in his neck and has no movement in his extremities. He will be going into surgery soon. On the back side of the piece of note paper Jorja used when Dan called, she writes,

> *fracture in neck.*
> *C4/C5*
> *Laminectomy.*
> *may not walk.*
> *vitals*
> *stable*
> *Dr. Clifford*
> *Surgeon*
> *Dr.*
> *Gina*
> *Martin*

Vertically, down the side of the note paper in big letters, she scribbles, "In pain?"

Dr. Martin says she will stay with Theo until surgery. She passes him the phone.

He sounds groggy and calm. "Hi, Mom. Hi, Dad," he says, as if he were about to tell us he had just been to the grocery store or bought a new pair of pants. The visit is short. None of us know what to say. "I'm okay. I'm about to go into surgery," Theo quietly says.

I choke out, "I will find us a flight, and we will be there tomorrow as soon as possible."

"Okay, I'll see you tomorrow."

"We love you so much," Jorja tells him.

"I love you, too. Bye."

Once again, the antiseptic click of the disconnecting line abruptly thrusts a thousand miles of endless Texas plains, New Mexico's vast mesas, and Colorado's towering Gore range between us and Theo's unknowable future. We wait. Again.

A few minutes later, across all that distance, an anesthesiologist appears at Theo's bedside. He releases a syringe into the IV drip. Theo drifts off to sleep. The surgeon, Dr. Kirk Clifford, finishes scrubbing while the gurney is being rolled into the operating room nearby and Theo is positioned face down on the table. Dr. Clifford pauses for a brief moment, bows his head, and closes his eyes.

At home, I flop into my desk chair, setting about to solve problems, not because I know exactly what to do, but because I do not know what else to do. "Who is this Dr. Clifford, and does he know anything?" I ask myself. Google's search engine reports that Dr. Clifford was trained at Yale Medical School in orthopedics and neurology. "Where is Grand Junction, Colorado, and how do I get there fast?" A direct flight on American Airlines gets us there by lunchtime.

We pack bags, not knowing how long we will be gone. I find out we can stay at the Rose Hill Hospitality House just across the road from the hospital however long we need to stay. I pen a brief email to work colleagues: "Our son Ted had a serious mountain bike accident. . . . The outlook is not good. We are glad to have him alive and breathing on his own. Beyond that I don't know."

Then we wait some more, in the dark.

At 4:00 a.m., the phone breaks the tense air again with its happy ring tone of light jazz. This would surely be the good news we were waiting to hear. Dr. Clifford tells us the procedure went well, Theo is in recovery, and he will be moved into the ICU. That is good news. Then it gets much worse. The injury is particularly bad. A portion of one vertebra has broken off and become embedded into the spinal column wall. His spine had compressed and twisted, pinching one of the spinal arteries. Another millimeter or two and the artery would have been cut off or burst open, and Theo would have bled out on the mountain. There is some bleeding internal to the spinal wall, which is alarming. He is fortunate to even be alive.

The surgeon has removed the bone shard from Theo's spinal column and has completely removed the back side of the vertebra to relieve pressure on the swollen spinal cord. He has also installed two titanium rods and six screws across vertebrae C4, C5, and C6 to stabilize the spine. "Based on my experience, it is not likely Theo will ever walk again, but he is a strong individual who will figure out a way to maximize his recovery and ultimately flourish in life, no matter what," Dr. Clifford says. "It is a bump in the road but not the end of the road." There is a matter-of-fact confidence to his tone.

We are unable to ask any intelligent questions or even to organize our thoughts. We thank him for his care to our son and hang up. In an instant, the air becomes stale, the lighting goes flat, food is irrelevant, and clocks are useless. Unable to absorb the news that something that happens only to other people has now happened to us, we desperately want to be there. We want to be there *now*.

Jorja lies on the floor in the bathroom connected to my study, clinging to the toilet, not knowing if she will throw up or pass out. I am certain this is the most vacant the soul of a parent can feel, short of losing a child to death. My mind floods with an onslaught of confusing facts, unthinkable scenarios, impossible decisions, and unanswerable questions.

I design wheelchair ramps into the house and look around for where the elevator to the second floor could go. I imagine myself in his body, looking up at the bright lights as the anesthetic closes in, wondering how I would wake up or even whether I want to wake up. I search "spinal injury" on the Internet as I take breaks to decide what to pack for an unplannable trip. Heavy medical jargon, talk of limited long-term survival rates, and low-probability recovery fill me with suffocating fear. I think, "God, I hope Jorja doesn't look this stuff up."

3

Theo's Journey to the Mountain

Theo's tendency to find danger began early in life. Our family stopped in downtown Houston on the way to the beach for vacation in Galveston, Texas. We were walking across a downtown street via a glass-enclosed bridge between skyscrapers. A small ledge and a chrome railing ran along each side of the second-story bridge. Theo, or "Teddy," as we called him then, was about two. Mae was an infant.

Running a few yards ahead of us, Theo climbed up on the ledge, squeezed himself between the railing and the glass, and pressed his nose and forehead against the window to watch cars whiz by below. When we caught up to him, he stepped down, and ran ahead to do it all again. The bridge continued into an atrium high above a bank lobby, but the glass wall stopped at the building entry. There was nothing but air between the railing and the marble floor of the lobby two stories below.

As we were about to enter the lobby, Theo ran a few yards ahead again. Out of the corner of my eye, I saw him step up to press his nose against glass he did not realize was no longer there. "Teddy, *stop!*" I shouted. He froze. He looked back and saw horror on my face. He dropped instantly to his knees and shuffled back to safety, saved in a moment from the unthinkable. That was the first time I nearly lost Theo.

Teddy, of course, is short for "Theodore." Before Theo was born, Jorja and I had been going through books of names for months, but nothing really stuck with us. We decided early on a middle name of Thomas, the maiden name of Jorja's mother, Betty. As Jorja's due date neared, we felt the pressure of finding the perfect first name. Sitting in the hot tub one day, listing names, one of us, I'm not sure who, said, "What about Theodore?" It somehow sounded right. It was strong and sounded nice together with the middle name Thomas. After we looked up its meaning, it was settled.

Theodore comes from the Greek *Theo-d ōros*, meaning "God given." As a bonus, it was a nod to one of my favorite historical figures, Theodore Roosevelt, who, only through his gritty hard work and determination, grew from being a sickly, undersized child to one of the most forceful figures in American history. When our Theodore was born on August 9, 1988, we were ready to write his name on the birth certificate.

"Theodore" seemed large for a twenty-one-and-a-half-inch person weighing in at eight pounds, four ounces, so we called him "Teddy." Teddy fit him well as a cute, towheaded blond with bright blue eyes. Generally compliant when it was time to go to bed or take a bath, he was intent on doing the right thing, something he grew less dogmatic about in his teen years.

Born in August, Theo was one of the youngest in his class, but he never seemed intimidated. On the first day of kindergarten, Jorja was dropping him off at the school. He paused and turned to her before walking into the school, sensing she was having difficulty letting him go. Theo cocked his head to one side, pointed his index finger at her with his thumb up in the shape of a pistol, pulled the trigger with a click of his tongue, and smiled and winked at her. He said, "It'll be okay, Mom." He turned and disappeared into the building.

We decided to go snow skiing in Winter Park, Colorado, as a family when Theo was six and Mae was four. I was the only member of the family who had experienced skiing. I learned as a small child while balancing on the fronts of my dad's skis. Jorja had never tried. I knew if you had a good day on the first day, you would want to come back. If you had a bad day, you would never be back.

Apart from being fully annoyed with their parents for overdressing them for the spring conditions, Theo and Mae had a blast. When we collected for dinner that first evening, everyone was full of stories, and a tradition was born. Snow skiing became our favorite family vacation. Ultimately, it evolved into much more than that for Theo.

When Theo was nine or ten years old, he made the switch to snowboarding. About the same time, he informed us that calling him "Teddy" would no longer be acceptable. Our next-door neighbor, Ted, had a pool, played the guitar, and seemed to have done just about everything in life. Theo thought that was all interesting. "Ted" suited him better, he decided, as childhood turned toward adolescence. It was only a matter of time before *Barney* and the *Teenage Mutant Ninja Turtles* gave way to *Pinky and the Brain* and *Johnny Bravo* in his cartoon-viewing habits. This pleased me.

Theo was then, and still is, what I would call a determined learner, never satisfied, always looking for some way to do something better. He worked hard, but this attitude led to accidents. As proof, I have a substantial file folder in my desk of insurance statements for stitches, sprains, and broken bones. One year we got a call from the sponsor of a youth ski trip that Theo had broken his arm. Another year, he called us to tell us an ambulance was taking him to Denver. He had a huge bump on his lower back very near his spine caused by a fall.

Some accidents were more avoidable than others if a little forethought had not abandoned him, like it does all teenage boys from time to time. I remember walking into his second-story room one night. His window was open. He had wedged his trombone case across the window frame, and he was rapelling on the outside wall above the garage and the concrete driveway with a rope he had tied around the middle of the case. This was intended, he explained, to get his blood flowing so he could concentrate on getting his homework done.

Theo was never one to take the easy or well-travelled path. He has always lived in the realm of the counterculture, cutting his own arc in life, choosing the difficult over the safe and relishing the challenge to prove something new to himself. Exhibit A is that, as a teenager, he decided to play ice hockey in Dallas, Texas.

He started late, after we had returned from my three-year expat assignment in France. Every other teenaged hockey player had a head start on him by about two years. He took beginner clinics, learning how to stop, how to skate backwards, how to handle and shoot the puck. Then he joined a team. His hockey playing was hard to watch at first. He was awkward, reeling and falling as he worked to control his body and the puck against the onslaught of the opposing team.

One night, during a game, he was skating along on open ice, watching for a pass from a teammate. From his blind side, an opponent leaned in and rammed his shoulder pad into Theo's rib cage at full speed. Like a rag doll, Theo recoiled from the violent blow. You could hear the loud *thud!* as the back of his head smashed against the ice. He slowly got up, straightened his helmet, and skated away with a dull, undaunted look on his face. He took some terrible blows, but he always got up and skated back into the game. He progressed simply through brute-force determination. At the end of the season, his coach presented an award to him as the most improved player on the team.

Ice hockey, however, was just a hobby. His college choice was guided by proximity to mountains with snow. We visited several schools around the country more as a formality. He decided on Denver University. On a typical weekend at DU, he and his friends would head for the slopes, ski from opening time to closing time at Breckenridge or Copper Mountain, and then catch a couple of hours of snowboarding at night at Keystone before stopping for pizza at Beau Joe's in Idaho Springs on the way back to campus.

By the time he was through college, snowboarding had become far more than a hobby. He saw it as essentially his expression in art. The way a painter sees a blank canvas and a composer sees an empty piece of staff paper, he saw an undisturbed slope on a fresh champagne-powder morning. Theo watched hours and hours of snowboarding videos on his laptop, picking up ideas. He always was trying something new, challenging himself with a cleaner turn, a new trick, or a bigger jump. Whether it was hockey, skateboarding, snowboarding, or anything else, he was not afraid of a few bumps and bruises if they meant getting better.

Once he left for Colorado, he would never return to Texas for more than a visit. Armed with degrees in international business and French and a minor in economics, he moved to Vail on the advice of some friends, where he was determined to find a job teaching snowboarding. He felt he would never get the chance again. He wanted to see what he could do there for a couple of years before shifting to a more serious career. Jorja and I admittedly struggled a bit with that decision, but in the end, we decided to support him.

Anyone who goes to Vail to teach snowboarding gets a second job to cope with the high cost of living. Theo started parking cars at the Marriott and followed his supervisor, Dan Miller, to the Ritz Carlton. Dan saw Theo as a perfectionist and thought he would raise the performance of everyone on the team. Dan laughed when Theo showed up at the Ritz the first day and said, "I want my nametag to say 'Theo.'" But Theo was serious, and it wasn't a request. So, from that day, he was "Theo."

Jorja and I first noticed "Theo" on his nametag when we were visiting the spring before his mountain biking accident. At the time, we passed it off as something probably intended to provide a level of separation between his work life and his personal life. Frankly, we put it out of mind as not applicable to us. On our next visit in August, we stopped by the hotel to ask for him. Nobody knew who Ted was. Somewhere during that time span, he changed his Facebook profile name to "Theo T. Krause," and his Instagram handle switched to "thearitstformerlyknownasted."

The week before Theo's accident, we spoke to him by phone. He mentioned he was going on a mountain biking trip to Crested Butte with friends from work. Both Jorja and I remember saying what we always said: "Be careful." Theo had a bit of a history. When we said, "Be careful," he always said, "Okay," and we all always meant it. No one believes anything bad is actually going to happen.

Theo was not too keen on the use of phones to call home. So much of the news about his life in Vail we gleaned from reading posts on his Facebook page. Most of his posts were about his general passions in life: snowboarding, biking, music, and food. A September 16, 2013 post read, "Oooeee! Headed to CB for a few days of mtb shredding. There will be a lot of 'shut up legs' and 'damn it, Scott dropped me again', as well as many a good time."

Mountain biking was never Theo's favorite sport, and it was not his best. Still, he could not pass up the chance to spend time with good friends in the outdoors. True to form, he was pushing out the boundaries of his limitations, working to improve his technique in the seconds before he was catapulted into the aspen tree next to a trail called Doctor Park.

Now, only hours later, as Theo looked up at Dr. Clifford telling him he would never walk again, the first thought that crossed his mind, which he did not intimate to the doctor until months later, was, "Fuck this shit. You don't know me. You don't know what I am capable of. I have heard stories about other people in this same situation. I choose a different outcome for myself." Months later, Theo would learn that when Dr. Clifford saw him the first time, the physician instantly identified with his patient. His first thought was, "That could just as easily be me."

Theo was waking in the fog of residual anesthetic the next morning when Dr. Clifford stopped in the ICU to check on his progress. Just before he left, Theo said to him, "Thank you very much for operating on me last night. I'm sure you are exhausted." Out in the hallway, Dr. Clifford struggled to hold his emotions, saying to his physician's assistant, "Here he is lying there, unable to move his legs and arms, unsure of his outcome, and he is concerned about me and if I am tired. In my entire career, no one has ever said anything like that to me."

By the time Dr. Clifford had left Theo's room, Jorja and I were already on our way to the airport.

4

The "Miracle Toe"

By seven o'clock, we were ready. Our pastor, George Mason, and his wife, Kim, appeared at our front door. Close friends Steve and Gail Brookshire arrived minutes later to shuttle us to the airport. Before leaving, we stood in a circle, holding hands in an intense moment. George prayed, "Help us remember who we become is not defined by the things we cannot do." These are the only words I remember. The trip to the airport was quiet—no one knew what to say. Silence was exactly what we needed.

The rest of the morning was like a slow-motion nightmare. The flight was annoyingly routine, as if no one appreciated the magnitude of the prior day's events. We forced smiles to the flight attendant, muttering a haphazard "thanks" as we sprinted through the door. Scott Everhart, an imposing 6'4" figure built like an NFL tight end and with a massive handshake, met us to taxi us to the hospital. After an interminable wait, someone buzzed us through the doors to the ICU.

Theo's room was quiet, disturbed only by the steady rhythm of beeps, whirrs, and clicks of the equipment monitoring his vitals or delivering medication. The room was sparse, glistening clean, with sky-blue walls. Eric Sjoreen was slouched in a chair that leaned back just enough to not be restful. Dan Miller was by the wall-to-wall picture window, seated in a recliner that opened into a lumpy twin bed for the night. The natural light flooded in through the window, accentuating Theo's pale face. The same window offered a color-filled panorama of the renowned Grand Mesa, the largest flat-top mountain range in the world.

An intravenous line snaked out from somewhere beneath the bulky neck brace resting on Theo's chest and shoulders. Another set of lines ran from his left hand. Two pillows were propped behind his head. He was wearing the ubiquitous olive-patterned hospital gown. Heavy, white cotton hospital blankets were neatly tucked around his sides and up to his chest.

Dan and Eric stood to greet us and introduced themselves in a whisper. The flurry of commotion awakened Theo. Jorja slipped around to the side of the bed, kissed his forehead, and told him she loved him and was so happy to finally be there. Groggy, he smiled weakly and said he was glad, too. I leaned over his bed and looked into his fearful blue eyes inches away, almost nose to nose. I had been thinking about what I would say in this instant through the entire flight. I said, "Ted. No matter what happens or where it ends, we will be here with you, whatever it takes. No matter how this turns out, the most important thing is that we will be able to say we left nothing on the table, we gave it everything we had. That's what we are going to do."

For the next seven days, the focal point of our entire existence shrank to a hundred square feet of sterile ICU floor tile, the stage of epic battles being waged in one bed to subdue the fear of what might be. Warm sunlight streaming through the window was replaced at night by harsh florescent light from the hallway creeping around the edges of the curtain pulled across a glass wall. Scott, Dan, and Eric traded spending a few hours of the night in Theo's room to give Jorja and me rest breaks.

A typical day was marked by the cadence of morning and afternoon shift changes of the staff. In the quiet, the methodical rhythm of Theo's leg circulation pump—gurgling as it compressed, hissing as it released—was hypnotic, comforting. The occasional, abrupt shriek of the IV monitor alarm sent whoever was nearest scrambling to press the "silence" button. Theo stirred from a narcotic-laced nap, usually complaining his neck hurt. Someone gingerly repositioned his pillow until it was just right. We might visit a little; he might eat something. Often he stared somberly beyond the wall. Tears would well in his eyes, and he would blink them away. There was no discussion about what he was thinking.

The hourly entrance of the nurse practitioner to take vitals and to force Theo to breathe into the spirometer was a welcome distraction at first, but it grew tiresome and especially obnoxious at nighttime. Mostly, we waited and worried. I tried to stay connected with my office, but frankly I did not care.

Emotions soared with each sign of progress and then plunged at every disappointment, slamming us back and forth between exhilaration and fear, hope and despair, like a loose wrecking ball swinging through the walls of an outdated warehouse. Every blow challenged the integrity of the well-structured life Jorja and I had assumed would stand forever. Rules or personal experiences to guide us did not exist. Woefully ill equipped, we could only decide or say what seemed right in the moment.

The room would snap to attention at the entrance of Dr. Slater, the rehabilitation specialist, or Dr. Clifford, the surgeon. We stored up questions for their visits hoping to get clear answers. The ambiguity of Theo's long-term prognosis was particularly maddening to me. The two doctors answered each question about potential recovery equivocally, reluctant to overpromise in a domain where plenty was known but not much was understood. What we did know was that his injury was "incomplete," that he was young, and that he was extremely fit. He was also exceptionally determined.

I obsessed over confounding technical medical diagnoses, confusing medication, and central nervous system jargon. Each signal of progress was quickly lost in the noise as I searched terms like "spinal injury long-term prognosis." The searches on his official diagnosis as a "C5" level injury and "Asia C" classification turned up ominous prognoses, such as the following: "Patients will need assistance with daily living, but they may have some independent function," or "patients are likely to have some or total paralysis of wrists, hands, trunk, and legs," and "patients will need assistance with most activities of daily living, but once in a power wheelchair, they can move from one place to another independently." I returned to planning where I would install an elevator in our house in Dallas so Theo could get to the second floor if he had to live with us. I even emailed an architect friend for recommended residential elevator companies. A ramp would be needed off the back porch, too.

In contrast, Jorja was clear-minded and focused. She set about the business of taking care of Theo. She did not cry and was not distracted by my machinations over the science. She regarded it as superfluous to the main task. She had the capacity to take what was given and rejoice in the moment, letting tomorrow take care of itself. I would swing into deep moods and cry, but she was all about what needed to be done now. I wanted more, sooner, afraid it might never come. Jorja was now on a mission, as though that deep cry on the first night cleared her spirit to allow her to do her job.

Theo's mindset was clear from the outset. Nothing short of full recovery was acceptable. Early signs of progress surprised everyone, including his doctors, but not him. I had a front-row seat to the brain's amazing capacity to reroute itself through different neuro paths to reach its target. Theo's biceps worked, and he could raise his wrists a little from his elbow. He furrowed his brow, pursed his lips to hold his breath, tightened his abdomen, and used every ounce of determination and strength to raise his right leg just a few inches off the bed. In the past, the same effort would have produced fifty or a hundred sit-ups. He could feel pinpricks in some areas but not others. We smiled at each other and gushed over each positive sign, mustering our most convincing encouragement: "That's great, Theo!" or "You go, Theo!" We cheered each time he reached a new mark on the breathing apparatus that indicated his lungs were strengthening as though he had shattered a new Olympic record.

Still, no movement was coming from his fingers and toes. Privately, I caught Dr. Clifford in the hallway, and I asked what that meant. Jorja was a little upset that I had not included her, but I did not want to expose her in that moment to what I expected as the answer. He explained that it was too early to tell. I wanted to know if Theo's hands would ever work again, and he explained that they were usually the last to come around. He had a couple of older patients who sustained similar injuries, and one was able to return to fly-fishing after his hands began to work, but the other had to have the fly rod strapped to his arms. "It's a marathon, not a sprint," we were told.

On day three, a newly awakened neuropath wiggled Theo's right big toe and delivered a jolt of excitement and hope. He named it his "miracle toe." Other encouraging signs appeared at an accelerating pace. By the fourth day Theo could raise both arms and wiggle a few more toes. Sessions with physical therapist Mark Huster were yielding results. Theo responded to Mark's positive but aggressive approach, and they resonated with their common interest in cycling.

The calls and texts to Theo's phone began to pour in as news traveled quickly through his community of friends. Emails and texts came from all over the world, including one from lifelong friend Ryan Parker, who was on a submarine in the Pacific, serving his country in the U.S. Navy. Flowers came from a friend in London. Messages from Singapore, France, and Chattanooga, Tennessee, arrived. He could not answer, though, unable to hold the phone in his hand, much less type or text a reply.

Theo's friend Christopher Jones posted a message on Facebook. He wrote, "The world around you, it is obese with love. We all have the time to share in your recovery. Let us be a grip to you, while you grip your strength & courage upon us, letting us know that we help you each day, to become healthier. We will be here in steps, in lunges, in leaps & in bounds. Each level of progress we will be at your side, with everlasting love."

When someone called, Jorja or I would hold the phone near his ear so he could speak with the caller, and each day, we reviewed the dozens of text messages, and he chose which ones to answer. Sometimes we typed for him; sometimes he responded using the voice dictation feature on his iPhone, but after reading and responding to two or three, he was too tired or too frustrated to continue, and we would stop. A side effect of his pain medication made him ultrasensitive to noise, and he could not bear to listen to a phone call for long. Holding the phone near his face gave him a claustrophobic sensation.

Occasionally, frustration with his limitations would boil to the surface in flashes of anger amid the cocktail of pain medication and moments of despair about his future. In one of those moments, his frustration escalated to an outburst after Jorja referred to him as "Ted." "Can't you all just fucking call me Theo?" he barked. "That's been my name for months. I've told you it's what I want to be called, and it shouldn't be that hard!"

"You're right," Jorja conceded calmly, without the slightest hint of a raised voice. "We knew you changed it for work, but we did not realize it was that important." The exchange memorialized the literal, as well as metaphorical, end of "Ted" and the emergence of "Theo," whoever he would become. Coincidentally, Theo's coworkers from the Ritz in Vail, the one group of people who knew him only as Theo, dropped off a care package and a "get well" card. The inscription on the card was a quotation from Khalil Gibran: "Out of suffering have emerged the strongest souls; the most massive characters are seared with scars."

Names, I was learning, had become very important to Theo. Memorizing and calling all people by their names was a skill he had been honing at the Ritz. In the ICU, he memorized all the names of all the caregivers, greeted them when they entered the room, and asked them how their day was going. This was a formidable task at St. Mary's, where staff rotated frequently through shift changes blurred by a medication-induced fog in

Theo's memory. From John, who came in to empty the trash, to Rachel, the nurse, the habit was not unnoticed. One nurse asked just after a shift change when he called her by name, "Theo, how can you possibly remember all these names?" He said, "It is my job to remember names. My only job is to get better and appreciate the people who are helping me." The same day, before her shift ended, Cathy, another nurse, stopped by to say that she was working in a different area this week. She had noticed, too, and she told him he had been an inspiration to her and the rest of the ICU staff that week.

A growing procession of friends passed through Theo's room. Jorja acted as coordinator. No other room in the ICU had this level of bustle and noise. He received an iced donut that was bigger than his head from a friend in Texas and a "hippie kit" from someone in Colorado, with various herbal and root-based teas, soaps, shampoos, protein-based milkshakes, and beet juice. Mae flew in from Dallas, bringing Theo a penguin pillow that would light up blue when you squeezed a flipper and Jim Gaffigan's book, *Dad Is Fat*. Some very tasty-looking cookies and chocolates arrived from his girlfriend, Maria Constanza Terrado, or simply Coni. Coni was in Buenos Aires, helping her mother tend to the affairs of her father, who had lost his battle against cancer three weeks before Theo's accident.

Coni's arrival at Theo's bedside was highly anticipated all around. Jorja and I had never met her. Theo had told us very little about her even though the two had dated on and off for almost two years. Theo and Coni met while working second jobs at the Marriott. Theo was a front valet, and Coni was a cashier. He noticed her. Too shy to muster more than a "hello" face-to-face, Theo invited her to lunch through a text message. Not completely certain who he was, she agreed to the lunch.

She decided he was at least interesting, somehow different from other guys. He was funny and passionate and had a worldview.

They began to see each other regularly throughout the season. Theo liked Coni's strength and independence. She shared common interests with him and was kindhearted. Both were also still trying to figure out who they were as individuals, which led to a six-month hiatus until friends encouraged them to give it another try. News of her father's cancer diagnosis arrived only weeks after she and Theo had reconnected, and she left immediately after the ski slopes closed in April to go home to Argentina.

In the days following Theo's accident, it became obvious that Coni was the one he most needed to see. The thought of her calmed him most as he lay there on the mountain, waiting for the rescue team, and he talked about her more and more as the time of her return grew closer, enough so that we began to worry about how she might react. The stakes were even higher for Theo, who saw her response as a referendum on his fundamental identity, his suitability as a person. When she saw him like this, she might decide not to risk the prospect of a future with someone who could need constant care, and she would simply sever the relationship.

Theo's fourth day in ICU was just getting started when Meghan (Meg) Cahill, Theo's roommate in Vail, picked Coni up from the airport in Denver. Meg had become a close friend to Theo over the past year. The afternoon sun was streaming through the window when Coni paused at the doorway, sheepishly scanning the room, as though she was assessing it for signs of danger, then landed her gaze on Theo. She dropped her backpack and walked straight to his bedside. She tucked her hand in his hand and hugged him lightly, but awkwardly, being careful not to disturb his neck brace. Theo wept.

Fixing on his eyes, she quietly declared with an unwavering but thick Spanish accent, "There is nowhere else I want to be. I want to be here, with you, no matter what happens." She did not break down and cry, and she did not hesitate in her words. Jorja and I, looking on, could barely believe what we were witnessing.

Coni appeared to us like an eighteen-year-old kid. She was petite, with long auburn hair and the signature dark brown eyes of her strong Argentinian lineage. Dressed in washed jeans and a loose suede jacket over a cotton blouse and a coarse woven scarf looped around her neck, she had a kind of a bohemian-meets-European hipster style. Her youthful look masked an old soul, and her kind eyes and gentle demeanor belied a fortitude we would discover only later. Still reeling from the loss of her dad, Coni had not had time to grieve. Her presence in the room brought an instant boost of optimism just when it seemed it was needed most.

Theo's body revolted the very next morning. The endorphin rush of survival was gone, the protective anesthetic from surgery fully metabolized. He had gained faint sensation to touch except in his hands and right arm. Unfortunately, this also meant he felt more of everything. Theo was in pain all day, mentally and physically, with splitting headaches, hypersensitive skin, and aching spasms. No position of his head against the pillows was comfortable.

To calm involuntary muscle spasms, Dr. Slater put Theo on a dose of Lyrica. It made his skin burn with hypersensitivity. He hurt everywhere. The doctor suggested Valium would relax him until his body could adjust to the Lyrica. The Valium made him hallucinate. After a fresh dose, he asked me if he was holding a bowl of ice cream in his hands. He was not. The only way he could maintain sensibility was to shut his eyes and listen to music through headphones because, he said, "Everything was too weird." Theo rejected the Valium after the second try and stopped the Lyrica, deciding it was doing more harm than good.

Later in the day, Coni sought out Jorja, who was taking a break in a small nook at the far end of the hall. A wall-to-wall window overlooked the same Grand Mesa in the distance. Pulling a wooden rosary from her pocket, Coni placed it in Jorja's hands. "My father gave this to me when he was in the hospital. I am finished with it. You take it now. You're going to need it more than me."

Six days almost to the hour from the accident, two physical therapists came in and helped Theo sit up on the side of his bed. He was upright only a few moments. His muscles fired to find an equilibrium, and he was hunched forward, unable to hold his chest up, with his chin resting on the neck brace. They led him through a few exercises, and he sat for a moment. Jorja walked over to the bed, cradled his face in her hands, and then kissed him gently on the left cheek. "I'm so proud of you," she whispered. "I love you." One of the therapists (Gwen, I think) raised Theo's arms up and laid them across Jorja's back. Theo said, "I love you too, Momma."

When he lay back in the bed, he said, "That was awesome." For Theo, it was a rush of sensations he had not felt in a week as his heart accelerated to push blood up his body. He felt alive. For Jorja and me, it was that first tiny glimpse of what might be possible.

Dr. Clifford came by the following morning to check progress. Theo performed some of his new tricks, easily moving his upper right body and hip. Dr. Clifford could not contain his smile. "What you are able to do today is just amazing. To be honest, this is where I thought you would be in three months, not seven days. I usually wouldn't say this, but I'm confident you will be able to walk." Dr. Clifford kept to himself his thought, "That just doesn't happen." Theo no longer belonged in the ICU.

Craig Hospital in Denver had admitted Theo into its rehabilitation program, but a bed would not be available for a couple of days. He was transferred out of the ICU into a patient room to start a little rehab work early. The physical therapist set him up with a wheelchair, which gave him his first chance to go outside. He also navigated a busy day of physical therapy and experienced gloriously mundane firsts, like holding a cup of water and feeding himself ice cream. With a little help from a Velcro strap to hold his toothbrush in place in his hand, he brushed his own teeth.

I was struck by the question I was asked while boarding a flight back to Dallas to take care of a few things at home. I was in seat 12C, the coveted exit row aisle seat normally reserved for frequent flyer members like me to further instill a false sense of accomplishment and therefore loyalty to the airline. "Are you willing and able to assist in the case of emergency?" a flight attendant asked. I had to gather myself to answer, "Yes." *Oh, God*, I thought, *let Theo one day be able to do something so mundane as to board with everyone else, not needing "extra time," sit in an exit row aisle seat, and answer, "Yes," to both parts of that question.*

I do not like to be in between places. When it's time to go home, I want to be home, not go through the trouble of getting there. I was in Dallas, and I wanted to be in Grand Junction. Theo was out of intensive care but not yet in rehab. When, for the first time, Theo was barely able to lay his right index finger over the top of his thumbnail in a demonstration of improved dexterity, I was in Dallas. Being away from the action was maddening. I called so many times that I annoyed everyone. "Do you mind if I take a bite, Dad?" Theo complained when I called during lunchtime. "Okay, Theo," I said.

Theo posted on his Facebook page for the last time from St. Mary's:

"So thankful, still again and again, for all the love that you guys are sending me. I can't use my hands at all, so I can't really type, or respond to messages, or make phone calls. Please continue to read my dad's updates every day. . . . Hopefully today I will get to cruise around a little bit in my new whip."

I worked on an "update" during the flight home, but it was one or two in the morning by the time I finished and hit the "send" button. The day had been extraordinary. I was just starting to ruminate the implications of Theo's accident, his rate of recovery, and the influence of the many people involved. I closed the update with a quote from a poem by Deena Metzger, which our friend, Karen Burns, had sent to Jorja. "Give me everything mangled and bruised, and I will make a light of it to make you weep and we will have rain, and we will begin again."

The hard work of beginning again, though, was yet to come. Jorja was with Theo in Grand Junction. Theo was waiting for a bed at Craig Hospital in Denver. I was in Dallas waiting to go to Denver, coming to the stark realization that this was something I did not know how to fix.

5

A Convergence of Strangers

F ixing things has always been a forte of mine. I get it
from my father. He was good at fixing things. Growing
up as the son of a poor Oklahoma wheat farmer, Dad
learned to fix things himself and taught me how to fix things
at home. Basically, you figure out how the broken thing works
by taking it apart, finding the root cause of the problem, and
putting the thing back together. One night, when I was a junior
in high school, I became the cause of the problem.

Driving home late one Friday night from the local pizza
place after a home basketball game, I rounded the bend into
our driveway, failing to account for the thin coat of ice forming
on the black pavement. With my steering out of control, my
bronze 1970 Chevy Impala slammed like a battering ram into
the support post between our two garage doors.

My grandmother lived above the garage and roused Dad out of bed in panic, asking, "What was that big bang?" He appeared quickly to assess the damage, wearing a "what have you done this time" look on his face along with his pajamas and a red plaid robe hastily flung around his shoulders, flapping in the frigid breeze with the belt dragging the ground on one side.

Dad was still in a full leg cast from a major knee replacement surgery. He hopped over to the post to assess the damage. Then, with pursed lips and fogged breath pulsing from his nostrils like a straining steam locomotive, Dad grabbed the nearby sledge hammer and persuaded the pillar back onto the foundation so the garage door could be closed for the night. Also in the business of persuading broken souls, Dad was the senior pastor at the local Baptist church, and to this day, I refer to every sledgehammer as "the preacher."

When I fix something, it is very satisfying—a victory of sorts. Dr. Clifford reacted the same way to Theo's progress. Although his repair work was finished on the night of the surgery, Dr. Clifford was particularly diligent in his follow-up visits. He understood the science of his field and knew he had done his best work. He genuinely rejoiced in the victory, marveling along the way at the body's ability to repair. He comfortably admitted that plenty was yet to be understood about the body's complex nervous system and that only time would tell the outcome. Nonetheless, he would show off the progress Theo was making to his colleagues like a proud father, dragging them into the room and saying, "Hey, watch this!" As a bit of a science guy myself, I understood that perspective very well, although my undergraduate degree in physics barely opened the curtain to a basic understanding of the enormously complex patterns of the physical world we inhabit.

When I cannot fix something myself, it is frustrating, even a little humiliating. The implication is that I am not smart enough to figure out how it works on my own. Something else was happening now, though, that I could not explain. In the case of Theo's accident, the struggle was immeasurably more acute. I am his father. It is my fundamental job to help, to protect, to "fix" my children's needs. But I was lost, so lost; I did not even know the starting point.

Strangers, despite having no relationship with or accountability for Theo or his future, without being asked, were nevertheless showing up out of nowhere to help at just the right moment, long before I even knew there was a problem to fix. Complete strangers, until our paths crossed, appeared to help a complete stranger in his most desperate moment of need, which, as far as I could tell, could not possibly be addressed better by any other person, including me.

Kirk Clifford was just one of these strangers. At the age of eight, he decided he wanted to be a doctor after he watched his dad, volunteering for the local ski patrol, work on an injured skier. Kirk, a long-range planner and active in high school sports, decided he would go to medical school, become an orthopedic surgeon, and return to Idaho to work in sports medicine. He was the first state college graduate from Idaho to be admitted to Yale Medical School. But one evening during his residency at the University of Iowa, while serving on a mandatory three-month "spine rotation," he came home and announced to his wife, "I want to be a spinal surgeon." Finding spinal surgery as his passion upended his long-term plan, but it opened a new path to Grand Junction where, thirty-six years after he first decided to be a doctor, he operated on Theo in the middle of the night.

Dr. Clifford was not the only stranger who came to Theo's rescue. The lone rider who found Theo on the mountain just after his accident was Farid Tabaian. Farid was one of few people in all of Colorado who knew every inch of the terrain. He had quite literally drawn the map. A native of Boulder, Colorado, he is the son of an Iranian immigrant who came to the United States to pursue his PhD in linguistics at the University of Colorado. Farid was on the mountain that day, honoring the memory of his mother, who died of cancer at the early age of sixty-four. Before she died, her advice to him was simply "Farid, follow your passion and do what you like."

He did not find his way to mapmaking until his mentor at the University of Colorado, Jim Rob, inspired him to pursue cartography as a career. Operating his business out of his home in Salida, Colorado, Farid meticulously crafts weatherproof, tear-proof mountain biking maps using detailed GPS data he personally collects. The day of Theo's accident was his thirty-third birthday, and, remembering his mother's advice, he took the day off to ride his favorite trail. Farid knew exactly where to go to find a cell signal and how to give the rescue team precise information about the accident site's location.

The woman who wrapped Theo in the heat blanket she retrieved from her backpack was Irene Rüesch, a trained nurse. Her longtime friend and mountain biking companion, Christine Landolt, who worked with Irene to keep Theo warm and talking, had just completed a refresher course to maintain her certification as a mountain biking instructor. The two Swiss Germans grew up in neighboring towns, worked together on the ski slopes, and shared a passion for mountain biking. Irene found her way to pediatric nursing after her original dream as a teenager to teach preschool was blocked by a dearth of apprenticeships. Christine likes to help people. Starting as a flight attendant for Swiss Air, she is now in her dream job, planning and leading mountain biking trips worldwide. Christine and Irene take annual vacations around the world, this year in Colorado.

Together, Irene and Christine knew exactly how to manage Theo's care until the rescue team arrived. They knew not to move him, that preventing shock and keeping him from slipping into a coma from a concussion was the priority. They massaged his feet and hands and kept him talking. Christine sat with his head in her lap, stroking his hair and reassuring him as a mother would do with her sick child. To Theo, she appeared as an angel.

Histories of major disasters, like Hurricane Katrina, Hurricane Harvey, 9/11, and the recent mass shooting in Las Vegas, are replete with beautiful stories of strangers helping strangers. The stories make it easier to believe that there is more good than bad in the world and that when it really matters most, people help each other. It seems reasonable to expect that when millions of people are suffering, instances of perfectly situated strangers choosing to help someone in need might occur. As Theo's rescue operation unfolded, this pleasant notion about human nature became very specific and very personal.

Eric Forsythe was the medical services chief at the Gunnison Valley Hospital who took the relayed call from the 9-1-1 operator. He had been on the job two years after finishing a nine-year stint as a ski patroller in Crested Butte. Eric could have taken a safe path into the family law business back in Ann Arbor, Michigan, but a new degree program at the University of Colorado in environmental economics caught his eye. As a bonus, he could simultaneously pursue his dream to become a licensed emergency medical technician. The combination allowed him to build a career in wilderness rescue and to travel the world, conducting specialized wilderness medical training for the Wilderness Medical Collateral Associates. Through this expertise, Eric Forsythe knew from the 9-1-1 operator's relay that Theo would require specialized, urgent help. He immediately called the Western Mountain Rescue Team into service.

The Western Mountain Rescue Team was formed in the 1960s by a group of Western State Colorado students after organizing a search for a missing physics professor, Rocky Rockwell. The organization is now the first college-based, nationally accredited Mountain Rescue Association Team in the United States, and it operates out of a dormitory basement as the primary search-and-rescue team for Gunnison County. Junior student Brian Larson, defying his boyish looks with unorganized strawberry blond hair and a wiry 5'10" frame, would serve as mission coordinator for the first time. Having trained for two years, he successfully managed a complex rescue operation and a team of twenty people to hand off his patient to the Care Flite paramedic.

Rob Weisbaum, the onboard Care Flite paramedic, likes to jump out of things and has never forgotten how lucky he is to be alive. At age twenty, in Detroit, he miscalculated a skydiving jump and slammed into the ground at sixty miles per hour. His feet were turned around backwards by the impact, and splintered bones were protruding through his skin. He had always wanted to be a firefighter, but marveling at the way the medivac team took care of him, he committed that day to become a medivac paramedic. Rob launched the operation in Montrose, Colorado, in 2009, and it was called into service to find Theo.

And Richard Westra, the pilot who skillfully landed the Care Flite helicopter on the bluff, is reminded every day of a helicopter crash three years before. Richard had not been expected to survive that accident. His wife did not survive.

The hospital staff at St. Mary's was also part of the tapestry. More than twenty people, from doctors to nurses to PAs to technicians to housekeepers, had been through Theo's room in the past week. Every caregiver on every shift was singularly focused on his recovery. Theo apologized to a nurse at one point for being particular about exactly where the pillow should be placed behind his neck. The nurse responded, "That's what we are here for, Theo. Whatever it takes to make you feel a little bit better, a little bit more comfortable. That's what we want to do."

All of these people, strangers all, happened to find themselves in the position to help Theo through the choices they made, often in the face of adversity, along the course of their lives. Farid happened to be cycling by; Christine and Irene happened to be on vacation. Eric, Rob, Brian, and Richard were just doing what they like to do and were there, as the medical system was designed to be. Were these perfectly equipped strangers there just by chance, all doing their jobs? Was Dr. Clifford, only by chance, on call that evening along with his top surgical team?

The premise "it just happened this way" fails my basic instinct to understand why things work. Alternatively, I find arrogance in the idea that Theo's good fortune was proactively orchestrated at the whim of some benevolent master of the universe. I could get behind the science of surgery and recovery, but neither alternative—that these things happened by chance or that they happened by design—was plausible to me. I only knew I could not fix it myself and I had not asked for any outside help. It came anyway.

Jorja was a step ahead. She said to me in the ICU hallway one day, "I was reading the twenty-third Psalm. I know now what 'you prepare a banquet before me in front of my enemy' means."

"What does it mean?" I asked. I had no idea where she was going with it.

She followed with, "I understand now about the 'banquet before me.' All these people, the exceptional doctors and nurses, Theo's close friend, all these people who are praying for us—this is the banquet table that has been laid out for us in this psalm by God to get through a time like this."

She just as well may have said, "It is a miracle." I was practically born on the front pew of a church. I was there every Sunday morning, every Sunday night, and every Wednesday night. There was a cooling-off period during college, but going to church has been a way of life for me. I've read all the stories and heard most of the sermons. Nonetheless, I cannot say I ever fully bought into the whole business of miracles as we have usually understood or explained them. Multiplying loaves and fishes and walking on the water were fun to talk about in Sunday school, and I did not doubt the extraordinary stories I heard about miraculous things happening to others, but I never personally saw one happen, and miracles did not affect my daily life. I received a degree in physics from a Baptist liberal arts college, but at no time did I bother to consider the sticky issue of science versus religion and how it applies to the concept of a miracle.

Only two days later, Jorja and I passed by two Saint Benedictine nuns in the hallway on our way back to the ICU from a short break. Jorja stopped them, explained Theo's story, and asked if they would remember Theo in their prayers. Sister Josie asked if they could come to his room to offer a blessing. Of course they could, Jorja told them. I abstained. Theo, normally not a strong proponent of organized religion, straightened in his bed when he saw them enter the room behind us but readily agreed to their offer of a blessing. The sisters stood by his bedside, one taking his hand. The rest of us completed a circle around his bed.

Sister Josie said a simple prayer asking for healing and for guidance for his caretakers. Then she touched his forehead, ears, lips, each hand, and each foot with holy water as she recited from the prayer "A Blessing for the Body and Soul." The blessing finished with the feet: "May God watch over you as you walk down your path of life and keep you safe from harm. May you follow the way of God." After a brief, silent moment, the two nuns left. I never saw them again. They came and left as strangers.

My father was good at fixing things, and I was no stranger to him. To those who were strangers, as a pastor he was often in the same position as Sister Josie, the sledge hammer replaced with a prayer. Had I been paying closer attention, I am sure I might have heard the thud of the "preacher" knocking our house an inch or two closer to the foundation.

6

Moving Day

The machines were disconnected; the IV drips were stopped. Theo passed the last evening in ICU laughing and cracking jokes with Jorja, Mae, and Coni, who fed him pizza for dinner. Mae reflected the positive outlook in a Facebook post to her friends the following morning: "This short pause today allowed me to realize not only how lucky we are to have Theo, but how lucky we are to have Theo in good spirits and to be able to surround him at all hours with a friend or family member." Mae quoted from a song she had memorized in the youth department at church called "Traveling Mercies" by Billy Crockett and Milton Brasher-Cunningham:

And for the faithful, and for the weary, and for the hopeful
This is my prayer . . .
Go in peace, live in grace
Trust in the arms that will hold you
Go in peace, live in grace
Trust God's love

Closing her post, Mae wrote, "I think of it as encouragement to Theo, I think of it as a thank you to all of the nurses
and doctors who have helped him so far, and I think of it as a
reassurance to me that He has it under control. I never knew
my brother was such a strong person." Mae, the spitting image
of Jorja at the same age, takes after her in other ways, as well.

Evidence Theo was experiencing this encouragement came
from his own Facebook post to his friends on what was expected
to be his last day at St. Mary's. He was in a good mood, resting
comfortably on the eighth-floor orthopedic wing. Still unable
to use his hands, he dictated to Siri, his iPhone's voice-recogni-
tion feature, "So thankful, still again and again, for all the love
that you guys are sending me. I will let everyone know when
you can start coming to visit me in Denver once I know the
strict schedule that the Craig Hospital will set up for me."

Jorja and I had never heard about Craig Hospital in Denver, but Theo had seen a 2013 documentary film, *The Crash
Reel* by Lucy Walker, which chronicled pro snowboarder
Kevin Pearce's extraordinary recovery from a traumatic brain
injury. Pearce, injured in a training exercise in Park City,
Utah, while preparing for the 2010 Olympics, was transferred
to Craig Hospital for rehabilitation. Craig Hospital has limited
space, though, and prospective patients are evaluated for suitability for its program. Theo explained to the representative

who came to Grand Junction to evaluate him for admission, "Each day I want to do one thing new, and do the old things better." Craig Hospital did not take long to decide there was room for Theo.

The plan was now finally in motion. Jorja was three hours down the road, more than halfway to Denver, in Theo's car. She needed to stop in Vail to pick up some fresh clothes for him and expected to get to Denver just in time to meet him at Craig Hospital. My friend, Doug Hill, was keeping me company on the twelve-hour drive from Dallas to Denver. I needed to bring a car and more clothing. We were preparing for a long stay.

One part of the plan was not in motion. So far, the insurance company had been spectacular in supporting Theo's needs, and we were thankful that a key early benefit of the Affordable Care Act, allowing children to stay on their parents' insurance policies until age twenty-six had ensured Theo was getting the care he needed, but the insurance approval to allow Theo to be transported from Grand Junction by plane to avoid the ambulance ride of over four hours had gotten stuck in the bureaucracy, waiting for the signature of a physician known only as "Dr. G. who was on vacation," Apparently, there was no backup. Doug was driving, so I could work on the issue.

I was already on edge, having spent a good part of the night before in my attic cutting off the electricity to a power roof vent that had started screaming at about 1:00 a.m. Unlike what was going on in Colorado, at least it was something I understood, something I could fix. I tiptoed across the rafters in my bare feet with a pair of insulated needle-nose pliers only to step on a loose low-voltage wire connection that set off the fire alarm, which in turn woke up our two dachshunds and generated a call from the alarm company. By the time I silenced the alarm and cut off the power to the fan, the dogs were snoring again. I was wide awake.

Now I was in the middle of New Mexico, having just passed the dormant Capulin volcano. Otto and Dietrich, the two dogs, were in the back seat, sleeping. As we climbed in altitude from Dallas to Denver, Otto was, shall we say, equalizing his air pressure from time to time, which had the one benefit of masking Dietrich's bad breath but also gave us a sense of what Capulin might have smelled like during its active years.

Doug listened to my side of the "conversation" as I prosecuted the insurance representative with what my friends and family know as the "Krause treatment." After I hung up, Doug said in his best slow Alabama drawl, "Now, Tee-um, you weren't va-rah nahs to that person. I thank you need ta a-pah-luh-jazz."

When I called again to find out if any progress had been made, the customer-care agent I spoke with delivered a powerful reminder that the voices on the other end of "press one to talk to a representative" are the voices of actual people, not just those of faceless "representatives." I was, by then, in full escalation mode and was being firm but cordial. At least, that is the way I heard myself.

The agent could hear my frustration. Before she put me on hold to transfer me, she said, "Mr. Krause, I want you to know that while we are on hold here waiting for this person, I will be praying for you and your son that he will be receiving healing right now and that you will find comfort." I doubt she was taught to say this in her training program, but it stopped me in my tracks like a thump on the back of my head by my mother for misbehaving in church. Nothing could be done about the plane.

By nightfall, Doug and I were in Denver. The plane was still on the ground in Grand Junction, and Theo was sitting in his room on the eighth floor. Jorja called to ask Theo how he was holding up. "I have no words to describe what happened here today," he said.

The next morning, one phone call between the hospital and the insurance company resolved the standstill. Theo had an uneventful plane ride on a King Air 200 to Denver, where he was safely delivered to room 314a at Craig Hospital. Jorja and I were there when he arrived.

The gesture of that call agent has lingered with me. I do not know her name. She probably said it, but I wasn't listening. I was singularly focused on my own situation, and she was not a real person to me, just a conduit to what I wanted. She may have taken twenty calls like that before mine, yet she chose to listen long enough to hear my need. She saw me, and then, she did something. She was yet another complete stranger in a lengthening chain of strangers. She saw a father's pain in my harsh words and shifted my focus to a sense of gratitude for the many people doing something good in a terrible situation.

7

Craig Hospital

As a first impression, Craig Hospital was not what we had imagined. When Theo arrived, he was wheeled into a semiprivate room on the third floor. The place did not look as if it had been renovated for twenty years. It was dimly lit with an institutional linoleum-tiled floor one would find in a junior high cafeteria and dull, beige walls with scuff marks and scrapes. Miscellaneous medical equipment such as a wheelchair battery charger, pushed up against the walls, and various adaptive attachments signaled he may have been moved into a room doubling as surplus medical supply storage for an underfunded government health clinic.

Behind the bed was a wall of shelving, mostly without doors, stacked with sheets, towels, clothing, and medical supplies. It was clean, but it was a far cry from the bright, modern ICU at St. Mary's. Adding to the ambiance, a jackhammer pounded away just outside his one and only window. We had followed the yellow brick road, and all we found at the end was a couple of worn-out machines, a hospital bed, and a curtain in a construction zone, which we later would learn was part of a $50 million renovation project.

To make matters worse, especially after the lost day in Grand Junction, nothing much seemed to happen the day Theo arrived. In the afternoon, a parade of physicians, therapists, nurses, and technicians sifted through to meet him, to explain their role in his care team, and to tell him that they had already heard about him and they knew he would be successful in their program. Theo made it crystal clear to each person who visited that he was ready to work and he was looking for whoever was the most challenging therapist to work with him. He told every doctor and therapist who came his way that he was tired of lying around and was ready to get to work.

Explanations that they had a methodical process to follow and that they needed to conduct their own independent tests were not convincing to any of us. Jorja and I did not say anything to Theo, but we wondered if we had made a big mistake. This was nothing like the ultramodern, top-flight rehab center we had imagined. Even the people were dressed differently. No one was wearing crisp, blue scrubs, and the doctors did not wear freshly pressed white coats with stethoscopes around their necks. Everyone was in jeans and sneakers or whatever seemed comfortable.

Leaving Theo alone that first night in an austere hospital room with strange people who seemed to treat his condition nonchalantly, as though it were completely normal, was as gut-wrenching as leaving a child at kindergarten for the first day of school or leaving the first child behind for their first year of college. He was twenty-five years old, a grown man in any-one else's eyes. One of us had been with him twenty-four hours a day for nearly two weeks. It was hard for us to let go and drive ourselves to the hotel for the night.

We did go to the hotel and eventually fell asleep after wor-rying extensively about everything that might go wrong in our absence. I am an early riser anyway, but Earth could not spin through its night cycle quickly enough for me. As I turned out of the hotel driveway just after dawn and headed west on Hampden Avenue for the ten-minute commute to Craig, my brain was spinning questions. "How had he slept? Was his call button where he could reach it? Had they come when he called? Did they turn him every two hours as they should?" I could not stand not to know.

I came over the crest of a hill, and suddenly before me lay Denver, the vast expanse of the western prairie, and the Rocky Mountains spanning the horizon as far as the eye could see. The morning sky was crystal-clear, and the mountain peaks gleamed in splashes of white from the first snows of fall the week before. Such a scene might have been inspiring on any other day. This day, I took it simply as the mountains' brash repudiation of accountability for robbing my son of his bright future.

When I tiptoed into Theo's room, he was sleeping peace-fully. A three-foot-long adjustable straw contraption stretching from his water bottle was attached by Velcro to his bed rail. The straw dangled about two inches from his mouth. He stirred and awakened from his light sleep as the technician came in to check his vital signs.

"How do I get one of these?" I asked. Without hesitating, Theo quipped, "Well, I don't think it's a good idea since your tumbler would be filled with something other than water." The night had not been perfect, but none of the doomsday scenarios we had imagined played out, and Theo was ready to take whatever the day gave him.

I did not make the connection until much later, but the straw was just the first sign of what the Craig Hospital treatment philosophy would be. The caregivers at Craig took pride in adapting their treatments, building special braces and tools, and innovating other solutions based on evaluating what the patient's needs were along the way.

We would learn that the caregivers dressed casually to give patients a feeling of normalcy. They interacted and responded in a relaxed manner, which not only reinforced the notion that the future was not lost but also encouraged the patients to begin to solve problems for themselves. They sought a balance to provide top-quality care without hovering. The longer we were around them and watched them interact and solve problems with Theo and other patients, the more impressed we became. The ultimate goal in their program was for the patients to transition to an independent life no matter their physical deficiencies.

The hospital buzzed with activity all day. Every Monday morning, each patient received a custom daily schedule for the week. The overstuffed third-floor therapy gym around the corner and down the hall from Theo's room was used for one-on-one inpatient physical and occupational therapy during the day. Standing machines, parallel bars, and floor mats were placed around the room, and every side of every pillar was packed with ropes, pulleys, tension bands, and other therapy equipment. Along one wall was a fully equipped kitchen used strictly for occupational therapy.

The gym converted to a dining room, complete with a buffet line for breakfast and dinner, as equipment was shoved to the corner to make way for folding banquet tables. Most patients brought their own chairs to dinner in the form of wheelchairs, so only a few folding chairs were spread around the tables. Elsewhere around the building were also classrooms for teaching music therapy, adaptive recreation, and other specializations.

The aquatic therapy pool was on the first floor, on the way to the Peak Gymnasium, an expansive and impressive-looking facility packed with a row of FES (Functional Electrical Stimulation) bikes, a Lokomat robotic training system for relearning how to walk, and a range of other weight-training equipment. This was the one place that looked as we had expected. Outdoors were stairways and ramps, a patio with tables and chairs, and stone pathways—all there to be used for practice in mobility, especially if a patient was fortunate enough to be in the gait or walking class.

The deliberate effect was that patients must learn to negotiate a maze of hallways and elevators to get through their daily schedules. Patients and staff rushed around constantly to get from one session to another. Schedules tightened as patients improved their ability to move from place to place. Most were pushing themselves in a wheelchair if their arms were working, and many more were in power wheelchairs. The whole production created energy with a sense of motion and of progress.

A small, manicured garden just outside the hospital's east wing had a pond in the center of it encircled by a meandering gravel walking path. It was the home of a modern metalwork sculpture named *The Healer* by Matt Clark. Matt spent two months in the ICU and six months in spinal rehab before doctors sent him home and gave him three months to live. Thirty-five years later, he works from a wheelchair.

The scrap-metal objects he used for the sculpture had all outlived their usefulness and were broken. He repurposed them for the piece. The inscription on the sculpture was a perfect summation of the philosophy of Craig Hospital: "My body has been broken and may not heal. But my spirit can and will transcend my limitation."

I have only one family photo from Theo's time in Craig Hospital, taken on Jorja's birthday. This garden is the backdrop. Mae, Jorja, and I are grouped behind Theo, who is strapped into his wheelchair with a white hospital blanket draped across his lap. He is wearing a flannel shirt jacket that belonged to his Grandfather Morton. We are all smiling broadly, although close inspection of Theo's eyes tells a different story, of one not willing to accept the premise of the sculpture's inscription, that the body "may not heal." I, for one, was clinging to its hopeful promise of spiritual transcendence with all my strength.

8

"I'm Gonna Stand Up Right Now."

Theo, I'm convinced you are going to walk out of here." Doctor B threw this statement out in the same way he might say, "Theo, I'm convinced that broken toenail will grow back." Doctor B had just finished his initial evaluation of Theo's neurological capability and had read the file from Grand Junction, which included background about his support system and his attitude. Most studies had shown that more important than functional return or rehabilitation is the support system around the patient.

"Doctor B" was actually Dr. Berliner. He had been assigned as Theo's rehab specialist, but we were confused as to how to pronounce his name. Was it "Beer-liner," which is maybe a plastic bag wrapped around a keg of beer? Was it "Berlin-er," like the capital city of Germany? Or was it "Bear-leen-er" as in John F. Kennedy's famous 1963 grammatically goofed quotation, "Ich bin ein Berliner," which technically translates as "I am a jelly-donut," referring to the Berliner, a famous German pastry. We were relieved to discover that most people, especially his patients, just called him "Doctor B."

"We try to play up the gains, but not too much," Dr. Berliner later confided to me. "But with Theo, we aren't afraid. He has big plans and big dreams. He comes to work every day and has a smile on his face. Maybe he is covering up other things, but he likes to work hard." Dr. B surmised that Theo, especially with the support of his family, would ultimately do well.

Theo was relieved he finally found someone on the same page with him. That morning, he turned his frustration from what he perceived as a slow start at Craig into personal motivation. He resolved in his mind that nobody else was going to work him as hard as he wanted to work. His personal credo became "no one except me is accountable for the ultimate success of my recovery." Work started the next day.

Physical therapy is so tangible. We could not see the swelling in the spinal cord going down, we could not understand or predict what might happen later, and we could not see the effect of the drugs or the surgical procedure. In physical therapy, we could see the work and the results. Seeing visible outward progress was such a welcome departure from the relentless ambiguity shrouding his spinal cord.

For Theo's physical therapist, Chuck Hammond, the underlying process is more nuanced than this. In the early stages of therapy, Chuck is intently focused on how a patient is motivated. "There is always a feeling-out period," he explained. "Each of us is always searching for who the other person is, and I have to determine motivations and learning styles so I can adapt." He found Theo to be a quick learner, focused, and highly motivated to improve. "It's a wonderful experience when that comes together and you figure out what will motivate them." Chuck sounded almost like a teacher.

Chuck had a positivity about him that was infectious, even for Jorja and me. We looked forward to every visit. I always hoped to run into him in the hallway because I would feel somehow reassured after talking with him. I asked him what drove his positive attitude. He said, "At Craig, we are all in a difficult environment. I put a smile on my face when I come to work, and I try to see the positive." His approach was a perfect match for Theo. Each day was exhausting, sometimes frustrating. Every morning, Theo had to decide to work hard again. So he insisted on having thirty minutes to will himself into a positive attitude, no matter how the prior day had finished. Chuck would show up, and they would disappear down the hall to work.

Our family craved a sense of return to normalcy, and Jorja's birthday offered a respite from the weighty issue of Theo's rehab. Mae flew back from Dallas. We did our best to celebrate, but it was hard to ignore the surroundings as we sat around the folding banquet table in the therapy gym eating carry-out Ethiopian food from a nearby restaurant. Theo's head occasionally disappeared from view, when his motorized wheelchair timer sounded to remind him to tilt it back to shift his weight. He looked as though he was going into a space-launch sequence as the soles of his white sneakers pointed to the sky.

The occasion reminded me of our first move to Paris in 1998 to start my expat assignment. We were sort of under siege, four against the world. We knew only a handful of French phrases, and we faced a bewildering set of logistical and procedural barriers. Sharing a meal together offered an oasis from the confusing world around us. It drew us closer as a family. The difference this time, though, was that we were broken, under attack from the inside.

Most patients move from a motorized chair to a manual chair. Theo never had to learn to maneuver in a manual wheelchair, though. He progressed so quickly that the therapists skipped the training, instead targeting him to move directly into the "gait class" for those who showed the potential of being able to walk again, at least at some basic level. Gait training began with exercises to strengthen his core and lower body. Then the program segmented the act of walking into its individual components of motion and developed each one.

Initially he was strapped into a "standing machine." Over time, the machine was set to place him in more and more of a sitting position until he could stand himself up from chair height. Jorja and I were taught how to attach a "gait belt" around his waist and hold it firmly, acting as spotters when he transitioned between his bed and his wheelchair. One morning, with no warning, he looked at Jorja and pronounced, "Mom, I'm gonna stand up right now." Meghan Cahill, his roommate from Vail, who happened to be visiting that day, said, "He just did it, and we all cried."

From the standing machine, Theo moved to the Lokomat. The Lokomat is a robotic training system that uses a body weight–supporting harness system over a treadmill to help the patient relearn how to walk. Two therapists were positioned on each side of him and were manually picking his feet up and placing them on the treadmill to recreate a normal walking pattern that his brain and muscles could relearn. A third therapist monitored his progress and could modify the parameters of the machine as Theo progressed. Over time, as his balance and coordination improved, the machine would allow him to bear more of his own weight. Directly in front of him was a mirror so he could see where his feet were landing and whether his arms were swinging in rhythm to produce a coordinated gait.

The exercise required tremendous concentration because he had lost all proprioception, his brain's understanding of where his left leg was in space. His right leg was also completely numb, and his left arm was essentially dead weight. He was forced to actively manage every element: how long his stride was, how high he picked up his feet, how he placed his heel first and then his toe, whether it was straight in front of him, and whether he was moving his arms in natural rhythm.

The morning I saw him on the Lokomat in the Peak Gymnasium, I discretely captured a short video clip with my iPhone because it was the first time I had seen him walking upright and moving forward. He caught a glimpse of me out of the corner of his eye, and I broke his concentration. He shot me a sharp "put that thing away" glare. I had crossed a line of privacy for him and created a distraction from pursuing his goal. He was also fighting an epic emotional battle of will and determination against his physical limitations. Adding to the frustration, Theo was taking strong blood thinners to eliminate a clot the medical team had found in his damaged left shoulder, and this was delaying the start of work on the left side until they were certain the risk of the clot breaking loose and entering the blood stream was gone.

The battle surfaced the morning Chuck took Theo to the third-floor therapy gym to do some standing exercises, where he stood for the first time out of the standing chair. To be brought face to face with one's own limitations is a humbling experience, and Theo found himself suddenly standing in front of a full-length mirror, the first time he had seen himself up close since the accident in September. With a high-protein diet and the increased activity, he was starting to regain some of the twenty pounds he had lost in the ICU, but all the tone he had worked so hard to build in the summer was more than gone.

His shrunken shoulders were rolled forward, his chest was several inches smaller, and his T-shirt draped over his body as if it were on a wire hanger. His bicep on his left arm was essentially gone, and there was a crater just below his left shoulder blade where a deltoid muscle had atrophied, now cut off from the command signals leaving his brain.

Theo stood there, staring in disbelief at a person he did not know, surveying his broken body from head to toe. Peering into his own eyes to find something familiar, he recognized himself, and he burst into tears, grieving as though he had lost a long-time friend. Chuck gave him time to collect and reminded him this was only a starting place. There was work to be done, goals to be met. The impact was one I think Chuck had expected. The session was over.

Whether Theo feared that this was the new normal or whether he was just stubborn, the experience flamed his motivation. Notes of encouragement also came at the right moment. We received emails from several of those who helped him in the first crucial hours after the accident. Richard Westra, the Care Flite helicopter pilot, emailed to give him some encouraging words and to tell Jorja, "It was my honor to give your son a lift to the hospital."

Robert Weisbaum, the paramedic on the flight, emailed to say he was tracking Theo's progress closely and told us, "Theo has remained strong, and I was impressed with his mind frame while we transported him. Clearly he is a tough man." Christine

Landolt, from Switzerland, wrote " Oh boy, you were so strong while I could just hold your head, hold your hand, feeling helpless and weak. You are a wonderful person, and I hope we will meet again some day."

The next morning, Theo gathered his thoughts and went to work again. Back on the first floor, next door to the Peak Gymnasium, Theo was lowered into the therapy pool. He walked. Yes, water is a favorable environment, and a therapist was helping him steady himself, but he walked. Theo, of course, was unimpressed and dissatisfied, wanting more. The next day, Chuck decided the time had come. He positioned Theo's wheelchair at the end of the parallel bars in the third-floor gym and gripped Theo's gait belt as Theo stood and steadied himself between the bars. He explained to Theo how he could use the bars as support and that he would pick one foot up and move it forward, then bring the second forward to land beside the other, and stop. Theo took his first, wobbly step. He took another and another until he reached the opposite end of the parallel bars.

We were not there, clapping, shouting, "Go, Teddy!" as we had been for those first steps he took as a baby. I was on the road to Kentucky to deposit Mae, most of her belongings, and her horse at a farm outside Lexington to start a new job. Jorja was sneaking in a few errands while Theo was in therapy.

I wished that cameras were rolling as a hush fell over the room, patients and therapists pausing to gasp in amazement. Instead, the victory was celebrated between Chuck and Theo alone, almost unnoticed. In a split second, those first steps became a minor milestone on a longer path, rather than the ultimate victory we all could barely imagine just three weeks before.

By Thursday, he had left the bars behind and shuffled about 75 feet with the help of a walker. Theo and Chuck counted out 150 steps. Theo still could not use his hands to write, so Jorja took dictation for his journal entry of October 9: "I walked. I cried."

Progression almost always followed the same course. Theo would surprise himself, and Chuck would move the goal post. Theo ended each day completely spent. Even on the weekend, when no organized sessions were scheduled and the gym was quiet, one lone cabinet was marked with a bright yellow Post-it note. Chuck had stuck it there, scribbling an instruction to the weekend staff: "Leave open for Theo."

While Theo worked, I began to wonder. Being in good company with the professionals, I, too, had no good explanation for the healing occurring in our son's body. None of the doctors or therapists who worked with him can heal anything. The best they can do is only promote healing. An injured biker can be medicated, stitched up, put in a cast, and given exercises, but the healing part is the exclusive work of the body. "Or," I wondered, "is something bigger happening?"

Was there a clandestine connection between the way the body is made to repair itself and the way the world around is involved? What was happening was miraculous to me in a mysterious sense. I was unwilling to declare it a miracle in the sense of divine intervention, something I considered possible but not very plausible. Maybe the miracle is found somewhere in the construct of the body, the web of people, the character of the man. Indisputable was that Theo, who was never supposed to walk again, could walk again.

9

The Copper Pot Brotherhood

Allll patients in Craig Hospital could use a little help from a miracle. At any given moment over fifty patients occupy the spinal injury floor at the hospital, and another fifty occupy the traumatic brain injury floor. All are in the same basic situation. Something bad has happened that will now alter their futures. The course they expected to follow has forever changed and will be radically different from what they had anticipated. They are all scrambling to regain a sense of normal, both physical and mental. The battle turns on the juncture of the past, "This should never have happened to me," and the future, "What will I do about it?"

I walked past a kid in the hallway one day who was maybe in his late teens. His head was leaning against a bumper attached to the headrest of his motorized wheelchair. Looking expressionless down the corridor, he controlled the movement of his chair with only slight pressure from a finger on a small joystick mounted on the armrest. A bulky breathing machine strapped to the back of his chair clicked and whirred as it forced air through his lungs. As I passed by, offering a weak smile to the woman beside him, who was probably his mother, I thought how immensely grateful I was that this was not the case with Theo.

No one, including Theo, leaves Craig without seriously considering more than once whether a viable option for "what will I do about it" is simply choosing to die instead of living. If the patients' sense of who they are has been so ripped to shreds by what they can no longer do, then they may easily convince themselves that they no longer serve a purpose in the world. No one carries more weight in this argument than another person in the same situation. The development of bonds among patients becomes an essential component of recovery. These patients naturally begin to exchange experiences about what happened over lunch or during group physical therapy sessions, and they encourage each other to spend more energy pushing forward and less time looking back.

Jon Atwater was one of about half a dozen patients, a sort of brotherhood who often could be found across the street from Craig at the Copper Pot Bar and Restaurant. The staff of the Copper Pot were used to waiting on Craig patients, so the restaurant served as an oasis away from the confines of the hospital where they could feel normal for a while. Theo was pulled into the group quickly because they appreciated his sharp sense of humor and admired his youthful determination. Conversely, Theo was drawn to their wisdom and perspective on life in the face of the tragedy each faced.

Theo and Jon met only a few days after Theo arrived at Craig Hospital as the two were passing each other on the sky bridge connecting the two main hospital wings. The bridge is much like the one in Houston our family was crossing the day we nearly lost Theo twenty-three years ago, with similar floor-to-ceiling glass on both sides. The Liniger Bridge to Independence connects the third floor of the West Wing, the inpatient section of the hospital, where new patients arrive, to the East Wing, the independent living section, where patients learn how to manage for themselves before leaving the care of Craig's expert staff.

The bright, airy sky bridge provides a sense of being outdoors, making it a popular place among both patients and their families needing a momentary break from the confines of the hospital room. On any given day, especially a sunny day, people can be seen just enjoying the view and the warm feel of the sun on their faces. Someone might be sitting in a wheelchair or on the floor to the side reading a book, or maybe practicing walking across the gentle slope of the bridge aided by a family member.

Theo was riding in a newly acquired motorized wheelchair, and we were enjoying the new freedom it offered. Jon Atwater was already living in the East Wing and was rolling toward us across the bridge in his manual wheelchair when he stopped us. He had already noticed Theo in one of the exercise classes. He wanted to introduce himself. He also wanted to tell Theo that he had seen him work and move and that he was confident Theo would walk out of Craig Hospital.

Jon knew what he was talking about because lightning had struck twice for him. In 1991, the same year we were vacationing in Houston, Jon broke his neck in a trampoline accident in Phoenix. He was also told that day he would never walk again, but he was only thirty-one years old, and everything went perfectly—from the rescue to his rehab in Barrows Neurological

Institute. He ultimately walked away. This time, his prognosis was less optimistic. He was surveying the progress on the dream house he was building in Durango, slipped off the edge of his second-story deck, which had not had the railing installed yet, and landed face down on the ground below, breaking the same vertebrae in his neck as the ones he had broken before, also the same ones Theo had just broken. Now in his fifties, he said, "All bets are off the second time."

The two guys quickly developed an easy relationship, and to be within hearing distance of them was to be exposed to the constant banter of their sarcastic humor. On Halloween, Theo could be seen going from room to room to cheer up other patients, wearing a replica of the pink bunny suit Ralphie Parker got for Christmas from his Aunt Clara in the movie *A Christmas Story*. Jon, meanwhile, had been to the basement to rummage through the leftover costumes, and he was now rolling about dressed as a woman with a rolled-up dollar bill stuck into his faux cleavage when Theo again met him crossing the Liniger Bridge. The encounter would not pass a test for political correctness, but it offered a brief respite from their serious work.

Jon canonized the day by capturing a video of Theo in the therapy gym. The video shows the backside of Theo riding an exercise bike, in the bunny suit, the white fluffy tail bouncing up and down in sync with each revolution of the pedals. Theo's right hand is in the air as though he is signaling a lane change, except only his middle finger is extended.

Outside the safety of the therapy gym, Theo was still confined to his motorized wheelchair the day a group of patients went on a field trip to the Denver Zoo. The outing happened three days after he had walked the parallel bars for the first time. He reluctantly decided to go only because a few friends were going. Charles Drahota, another member of the Copper Pot brotherhood, was one of them. Charles is one of those guys everyone wants to hang out with just to see what might happen next because he has done just about everything. He is a story-teller and a lover of life.

Maybe because he was born eight years after his older sister and spent the better part of his early years hanging around the Seventh Street Bar his parents owned, he has always figured out a way to recover and thrive. As he explains it, "I always go out and do crazy shit." He has an unlimited library of funny stories, but the only thing he remembers about his accident is coming home drunk, walking up the stairs, and tripping on a step. The surgery he had in Steamboat the next day was his twenty-third. When you are with Charles, living is a good thing. He is going to make you laugh at some point.

Earlier, Charles warned his therapist he had decided the zoo was the place he would step up out of his chair and walk inde-pendently for the first time. He loves the zoo because he loves animals, not that he just wants to look at them and pet them. He also likes to shoot them. "I take pictures of them, and I harvest them," Charles said. "I have twenty-two African mounts."

Theo was nearby when Charles stopped his chair. The ther-apist set the brake and positioned himself to the side as a spotter in case Charles stumbled. Charles rose gingerly from the chair, at first bearing most of his weight on his arms, then stand-ing. He steadied his balance and stepped forward, walking ten paces around a monkey cage before returning to the safety of his chair.

A lone entry in Theo's journal for that day makes no men-tion of Charles. It says only, "Went to the Denver Zoo. Felt a kindred spirit with the animals confined there. They're stuck looking pretty in cages while I'm stuck in my own body." Theo and Charles had become competitive in the gym, seeing who could best the other on any given exercise. Theo confided to Charles part of what drove the competitive spirit, telling him, "When you were at the zoo that day I thought, 'I'm never gonna let that old fucker outdo me.'" Charles laughed, but for Theo it had been a life-versus-death-decision moment.

"Theo is a big inspiration for me," Charles told me. "He is my most valuable person in this place. He works so hard it inspires me." He recalled Theo coming into the gym and pronouncing, "Charles, that's the first time I've pissed standing up." Charles responded to him, "You know, it's the small things."

"He is a perfect example of not taking life too seriously," Theo said of Charles. "He has limitless energy. He never gets too sentimental. He's a little afraid of that because his life is built on fun."

Charles was a motivating force for his differences, but Theo wanted to be like Jon Atwater. Like Theo, Jon fell in love with the mountains and skiing at an early age. He also likes beer, which he enjoyed brewing in his bathtub. He enjoyed it so much that in 1990, armed with degrees in biochemistry and molecular biology as well as a PhD, Jon left his postdoctoral work at the Salk Institute in cancer research to open a microbrewery in San Diego in partnership with a friend. Jon will tell you their "Red Roost" beer, a hoppy ale, was the brewery's biggest achievement. One year after opening the brewery, he was paralyzed in the trampoline accident. Three months later, he was back brewing beer, still wearing a halo attached with six screws into his skull. In 1992, he walked the full 5K portion of a half-marathon event in La Jolla with his wife, Jenny.

When the microbrewery market began to soften and some cracks formed in the partnership, Jon and his partner sold the brewery. Jon started teaching part-time at a local community college and eventually went to full-time teaching at Southwestern College. Jon and Jenny bought the land in Durango in 2003 when their daughter, Hannah, was only three years old. They camped on the property every year, and Jon started building the house. It was about 90 percent finished when he fell off the deck in 2013.

When Jon told Theo his story that first day they met on the bridge, Theo was captivated by Jon's attitude. As Theo described him, "Jon's heart came out through his smile. He had the life I dreamed, with a wife, a kid, and a second house in Colorado. I believed everything he said because he showed so many signs of being like me in my ideals and my way of thinking."

Jon, Charles, and Theo, as well as every other patient around the table at the Copper Pot, sat down as complete strangers under tragic circumstances. The Copper Pot is gone now. Jon lives in California, teaching in a total fitness program called "The Unbeatable Mind." Charles lives in Montana but returns to Craig every year for more therapy and to show patients there what is possible. "The world needs someone like you," a patient's husband recently told him. The unlikely brotherhood they formed to overcome an unimaginable situation left an indelible mark on each of them, on the world they live in, on my son, and on his family.

10

Just Seventeen Steps

Twentieth-century mathematician, poet, and inventor Jacob Bronowski said, "One aim of physical sciences had been to give an exact picture of the material world. One achievement of physics in the twentieth century has been to prove that aim is unattainable." The concept could not have been more on display than the day of Theo's first "Family Conference."

Theo was becoming a bit of a celebrity by this time. Inside Craig, onlookers encouraged him as he methodically walked past. His right hand gripped one rail of the walker; his left forearm settled into a makeshift armrest and handgrip fitted on the other rail by a technician. Jorja or I would have a firm grip on his gait belt. Just as Chuck had shown him on the first day at the parallel bars, Theo took one step in the walker, checked his balance, and brought the other foot forward to a standing position. He repeated the action, each time starting with the opposite foot. The motion resembled the classic step-stop-step of a bridesmaid proceeding down the aisle at a church wedding. The biggest challenge was to properly place his left foot, which occasionally dragged as it came forward or was too far out or too far in.

The medical staff walked a tightrope, wanting to encourage and congratulate Theo but not to demotivate other patients looking on, who might never have that experience and needed to remain focused on goals of their own. Even Theo was developing a sort of "survivor's guilt," feeling unworthy that he was the one making all the progress. "Why is this happening to me?" he wondered. "And not someone else who deserves it more?" Nonetheless, he stayed quietly focused on his end goal.

The morning of the family conference, Theo was ready for his breakfast when I walked into the room. I went to the kitchen to pick up some scrambled eggs, brought them back into the room, and set them in front of him. He naturally picked up his fork like a normal person and began to eat. "Theo!" I said. "Since when can you use your fork without an aid to strap it to your hand?"

"Well, since this morning. I was hungry and wanted a bite of my yogurt. I didn't want to wait for someone to bring me that strap so I just picked up my fork and started eating." Just then a text message alert chimed on my phone. It was from Mae, saying, "You need to look at your mail." So I looked at my mail. She had accepted a formal job offer from SmartPak in Plymouth, Massachusetts, would be looking for places to live, and hoped to start in two weeks. My kids could not be more different from each other, but they do share a few key qualities. They have always chosen their own unique paths, and when they see something they want to do or achieve, they just set about to make it happen. Smartpak had been Mae's top pick for a place to work since the beginning of her search. Theo just wanted some yogurt. Both cases provided a powerful reminder I had no influence over the outcome. I had clearly lost control.

The "family conference" just after lunch was an intimidating affair. All the members of Theo's care team were assembled, quietly seated on one side of the table, facing Theo, Jorja, and me on the other side. Reading notes from a prepared report, each member gave a view of Theo's injury and progress and recommended next steps. The group included two specialists: Dr. Shi-Fong (Mike) Hsu, who would be retiring at the end of the month after forty years of practice, and Dr. Berliner, who was guiding Theo's case through to the finish. The two doctors gave their own detailed perspective of Theo's injury and the surgical repair, referring to elaborate photos of fresh scans of his neck projected onto a screen. Theo's physical therapist and occupational therapist talked about what they had observed and wanted to do next. His psychologist discussed the balance between a positive attitude and the necessity of grieving for what was lost.

Theo's primary spinal doctor, his OT, and his PT all started their reports in about the same way: "Theo, first, I have to tell you what a privilege it is to get to work with you." Chuck Hammond said, "When you first got here, it took us a few days to catch up with you." In fact, Theo had to correct both Chuck Hammond and Maureen, his initial occupational therapist, on their progress reports with improvements he had made in their absence over the weekend. Theo further informed Chuck he needed to be cleared to use other various machines in the gym because nothing was happening on the weekend, and Theo needed to be in there using them. Theo also asked for his mom to be certified to help him into the "standing machine" because he expected to be eating all his meals standing up.

The truth about who controls anything really surfaced as the meeting closed when Dr. Hsu, his initial spinal specialist, who had been a pioneering force at Craig for decades, said, "Theo, let's be clear. We are not actually doing anything here to heal you. The body is doing all of that by building and learning new paths. That's why we don't know how this will turn out. But when it gives us something to work with, we can help." So Dr. Hsu, like me, also had no control. For me, the sheer volume of medical expertise and focused attention being brought to bear for his benefit was proof enough we were dealing with a life event for Theo far, far beyond my influence. The session ended with the team revising Theo's estimated release from the inpatient program to November 19.

Immediately after the family conference, I had to leave for the airport for a long-scheduled business trip to Rio de Janeiro. Before leaving, I asked Theo how he thought the conference went. "Oh, about like I expected," he said. "I knew all of that stuff, and it doesn't affect me much. It may take a little longer than I thought, but I know what my goal is."

Concentrating on the work ahead was fruitless, and sleeping was impossible on the long overnight flight as the shocking events of the last few weeks, the readouts from the family conference, and Theo's answer cluttered my thoughts. When I arrived, bleary-eyed and jet-lagged, for a meeting at the hotel in Rio the next morning, I was surprised to find many of the people in the local team there had been reading the updates I was sending. They wanted an update on Theo.

Brazil is a highly religious society, about 90 percent subscribing to some religious ideal. The country has the largest

Roman Catholic population in the world. Without my knowing, the meeting organizer had arranged for me to take a half day to visit several sites in Rio, including the famous Christ the Redeemer statue. I tried to back out. "You need to do it," said the people in the local team. "We insist." It was a foggy, rainy day, so Luis Tonisi took me first up the cable car to Sugar Loaf Mountain, where we could see Rio and hopefully catch a glimpse of the statue on Corcovado Mountain in the distance.

For a brief moment, the statue peeked out from behind a hole in the cloud cover, but it was gone quickly. Luis, believing nothing happens by chance, insisted we go to the statue anyway. He drove us the long way through Copacabana. I hummed Barry Manilow's 1978 song by that name, which is actually set in a New York City nightclub and connects to Cuba. We then crept through the stop-and-go traffic in Ipanema, where I kept an eye out for a girl who was tall and lovely, before we left the city and began the climb up Corcovado.

I had a little motion sickness by then. I wondered how I would fake my appreciation for this trip up a windy road to a kitschy soapstone and concrete statue I probably would not see, anyway. Besides, what could be bigger than the fifty-two-foot-tall Big Tex at the Texas State Fairgrounds exclaiming, "Howdy Folks!" every hour in his booming voice? We arrived at a lower parking lot and transferred to a van, the only way we could get the rest of the way to the statue. The thick fog still shrouded the mountain, but it had begun to thin, and the day was brightening.

The van dropped us at the foot of a path leading to a cascading series of staircases. As we made our way up the stairs to the top, arriving just below the base of the statue, the clouds parted, and there loomed this massive statue of Christ, a hundred feet tall atop a twenty-five-foot pedestal, with outstretched arms spanning ninety-two feet. The entirety of Rio with its 16 million people was sprawled below, held down by the steep, green, jungle-draped mountainside and captive against the sparkling, aqua Guanabara Bay beyond. To the other side, the mountains plunged dramatically into the South Atlantic Ocean, which then disappeared into the distant horizon.

Overwhelmed by the vastness of the scene, I could not keep tears from gathering in my eyes. To regain my composure, I busied myself identifying landmarks below. Out of other things to find, I turned away, toward the Christ. I removed the purple rubber bracelet, which was inscribed with, "I'm a Theo" on one side, and "Band of Theos" on the other side from my wrist. My brother Philip had had a bunch of them made up just after Theo was injured, and we passed them out to friends or anyone else who wanted to wear one as a symbol of solidarity. Dozens of people wore them for months, and the bracelets began to appear in photos taken all around the world and posted on Theo's Facebook timeline.

I placed the bracelet on a railing in front of the statue and snapped a picture with my iPhone, slipped the bracelet back onto my wrist, and stared up at the face of the Christ for a while. One of the hardest things to come to terms with as my children have successfully escaped the talons of parenthood is that there are fewer and fewer things I can fix or provide for them. Maybe, like some of my home-improvement projects, I was never as good at parenthood as I had thought, and that it works at all, despite my meddling, is a testament to the engineering that came before. On this one, I was out of fixes, and I could only pray that this Christ represented a God with a very, very big sledgehammer.

Tears now flowed uncontrollably as I prayed words I do not remember today. Luis Tonisi reflected on his experience watching my struggle in an email to me later: "I cannot forget when you saw the big statue of Christ with the beautiful landscape of Rio behind you and started to cry, holding the Theo bracelet and praying for your son. I felt so much energized looking to a father, not to a key executive of my company, but to a father who really loves his son and family and for a few minutes who had the opportunity to meet God materialized in a statue where they both could talk and pray for Theo."

While I was climbing the stairs to see Christ the Redeemer up close, the mundane business of miraculous healing continued three floors above Matt Clark's statue at Craig Hospital. Theo's left hand had still shown no signs of life—except for his middle finger. I don't know what meaning should be taken from that. I posted something pithy about this fact on my Facebook page, and ninety-year-old church member Dot Laux commented that, the day before my post, she had been praying for Theo's recovery, as she did every day, and had decided to paint the middle finger on her left hand with purple fingernail polish.

On Saturday, I was back in Denver. I went immediately to the hospital to catch up with Theo, but he was nowhere to be found. It turned out he had convinced a therapist to open the pool on the weekend and convinced her to come spend an extra session with him. When I finally found him, I could not believe the progress. His overall strength and endurance were noticeably better. Still with the use of a walker, his gait had smoothed. Walking through the halls of the spinal-injury wing with him was like being at a cross-country racing event. Regular cheers of, "Whoop-whoop!" and "You go, Theo!" from patients and staff followed him as he strolled by.

Jorja shot a video to send to Mae of Theo and me that afternoon walking across the sky bridge. I still kept my hand tucked firmly into his gait belt. He still wore his neck brace. He had been instructed to wear it longer than average because the doctors and therapists are more conservative with patients who recover more quickly. As he strolled by the camera, he exclaimed with a big smile, "Hey, Mae! Check me out!" One lab tech, Christina, stopped to say, "You've inspired me today, Theo."

That evening, he put on his jeans and a nice sweater. Theo was cleared to leave the hospital grounds without wheelchair support. We climbed in the car and went to dinner at Undici's, a nice local Italian restaurant just down the street. The restaurant staff were accustomed to hosting patients from Craig Hospital and welcomed us without fanfare, without any second glances into the spacious dining room, as though we were a normal family out on a normal evening just wanting to have a nice dinner together.

Five days later, I came back to the hospital from our apartment after lunch to find Chuck and Theo out walking down the sidewalk together. Theo had a brace on his left knee to stabilize its movement, his neck brace was in place, and Chuck had a hold on the gait belt, as usual. The walker was gone and had been replaced by a crutch in Theo's right hand. They were practicing walking on uneven pavement and stepping on and off the curb.

This was a nontrivial exercise while Theo was still learning to replace lost reflexes with visual cues. The only way he knew that his foot had cleared the curb and had landed safely on the sidewalk was if he saw it there. His walk was uneven, and his arms moved awkwardly in a mechanical response reminiscent of the original C-3PO humanoid robot from *Star Wars*. Still, it was hard to imagine that less than three weeks had passed since he had taken that first wobbly step between the parallel bars.

Having Theo step up and down from the curb was Chuck's way of beginning preparations for Theo to tackle stairs. He knew that stairs were a very big issue for Theo. His apartment back in Vail had seventeen steps from the parking lot to the front door and another seventeen steps from the first floor, where his bedroom was located, to the second floor, where the kitchen and living room were. The steps from the parking lot to the front door would usually be covered with ice and snow, and we worried about whether he would be able to continue living there.

I had already spent numerous sleepless nights designing the elevator into our home in Dallas or figuring out where we could move him so he did not have to negotiate flights of stairs. The time I had wasted designing wheelchair ramps and installing accessible doors and countertops did not deter me from this sacred right of a parent to worry.

Most of the time, Theo was ready to try anything Chuck suggested. Chuck was careful not to push Theo beyond his limits, always looking for ways to create a situation for success. He also knew he had more latitude with Theo. He told me once, "I didn't have to be a cheerleader with Theo. He had the self-discipline."

Sometimes, though, the therapist must push. Theo was afraid, but Chuck knew he was ready. As Dr. Seuss said, "Today is your day, your mountain is waiting, so get on your way." Through the steel door with the overhead sign labeled "Stairs" they went. "Up with the right, down with the left," Chuck explained to Theo. This approach put most of the responsibility onto Theo's strongest leg in both directions. The left hand would grab the bannister, and the crutch in his right hand would track with his weak left leg, creating an opposing balance.

They started up, Theo's heart pounding, fearful he would fall and break his neck again. Chuck gripped the gait belt. Theo grabbed the bannister and stepped up with his right foot, then pulled his left foot and the crutch to the same step. Success. Again. And again. And again. And a flight of stairs was done. They turned around. Chuck stood beside him, gripping the belt. Theo grasped the bannister with his left hand.

The stairs looked much steeper going down than going up. His core tightened, and his right leg held steady as he lowered his left leg and the crutch in his right hand to the stair below. He planted his foot firmly and brought his right leg even with it. Success. Again. And again. And again. Back to the landing at the doorway. Theo has never ridden an elevator since unless it was inconvenient for others. "Why take the elevator," he asks, "when I can use the stairs?"

11

The Fight For "Normal"

Time was limited for Caitlin Glennon, Theo's occupational therapist, to prepare him for independent living. His projected discharge date from inpatient care had been accelerated twice. While Chuck, as his physical therapist, was primarily occupied with mobility, Caitlin focused on activities of daily living, like bathing, cooking, eating, and buttoning a shirt. Occupational therapists help the patient break the activity into individual tasks and strengthen a muscle, teach them an alternate approach, or provide them a tool to aid a task. "It's a hard line to walk," Caitlin says when speaking about how hard to push a patient. "Patients often return to Craig later and say I didn't tell them how hard it would be. You prepare them, but you don't want to add to the anxiety they already feel."

The work is in Caitlin's bones. Her mother is an occupational therapist. As a child, after daycare, Caitlin passed the time at the nursing home in Wisconsin where her mother worked, practicing various procedures she had seen, like making splints for her own little fingers. When her mother moved to the school district to work with children, Caitlin made friends with the students. She became an integral part of helping her childhood friend, Aaron, confined to a wheelchair from a spinal injury, learn how to manage daily life. Caitlin was in her fourth year at Craig Hospital when she became Theo's occupational therapist.

Throughout his rehab, Theo rejected almost every offer to use some sort of tool as an aid. Early in the process, when he was getting just enough function in his right hand to scoop food with a fork but could not hold a knife or a piece of bread with his left hand, he accepted the use of a sort of food backstop tool for his dinner plate. The tool was a curved sheet-metal strip about an inch tall and six inches long and affixed to the back side of the plate. He could push his food against the tool to trap it onto his fork or into his spoon. He only reluctantly accepted any tool that would help him button his shirt or tie his shoes to shorten the time to get ready if he was running late. He was determined to learn these tasks again on his own, always with the expectation that, at some point, he would be able to perform them normally.

Theo placed a high priority on one activity: cooking. Discussing their work plan, Caitlin agreed to schedule a session for Theo to make his own breakfast. He would go to the store, pick out and purchase the ingredients, and prepare his meal in the third-floor therapy kitchen. He was excited about this the night we took him to the store to pick out everything.

He decided the first meal would be a simple protein shake. For most, this would mean putting a couple of ingredients into a blender and pressing a button, but Theo is a foodie, and whether he is making scrambled eggs, a protein shake, or a chocolate soufflé, it is going to contain a little something special. He selected six ingredients for his shake, including various superfoods, fruits, and spices. In the kitchen, he worked diligently to formulate his concoction within the time limit of the session, but it was taking much longer than he had expected. Something as simple as removing a lid, he discovered, was complicated. His frustration grew. At last, the blender stopped, and the shake was complete. He poured the concoction into a cup.

"I'm always wanting to make the perfect challenge," Caitlin explained to me later, "not too easy and not too hard because I don't want them to get down on themselves." Theo worked extremely hard and made the shake. He picked up the cup, but, just before he could take a first sip, it dropped through his hand to the floor and splattered all over his shoes and his shorts. He stared down at the mess in furious disbelief, looking as though he was about to cry. Caitlin stepped in quickly to take the blame, saying, "This was not the right challenge for this day, Theo."

As he stood surveying the damage, she suggested they just stop. She would get the mess cleaned up. Theo would not allow it. His temper flared. "If I'm going to live on my own, I have to learn to clean up my own mess!" he barked. Awkwardly dropping to the floor, he spent much of the next hour on his knees, stubbornly mopping up. Caitlin was used to absorbing the frustration. "It comes with the territory'" she said, "as someone realizes for the first time the difficulty to do simple things like tying a shoe string." She had never seen this level of obstinate determination. She paused and shook her head as she played the scene back in her mind. "This one was an experience I will never forget."

One week before Theo was discharged from inpatient care, *USA Today* told the story of thirty-two-year-old Tim Bowers, married just three years, who fell out of his deer stand one Saturday, crushing the same vertebrae in his neck that Theo had injured. When Tim was awakened from an induced coma in the hospital on Sunday morning, he was told he might be on a breathing machine the rest of his life, might never walk, and might never be able to hold the baby his pregnant wife was carrying. Determined he did not want to be confined to a wheelchair the rest of his life, he directed the breathing apparatus to be disconnected, and five hours later he was dead.

As Theo was being prepared for surgery that awful night almost eight weeks before, he received similar news. Like almost every other spinal-injury victim, he was having similar thoughts. In a matter of milliseconds, he went from being in the best physical condition of his life to being millimeters from never being able to feed himself, or worse. Most of the predictions were wrong. Even Dr. Hsu, who had predicted Theo would "be left with serious deficits," conceded Theo was progressing much faster than he had predicted.

Late on the morning of November 19, Theo was dressed, wearing tan jeans and a light gray Mishka brand sweatshirt with "Engineered to Destroy" boldly printed across the chest. The clothing company's website says, "Anyone who has the passion for the unusual, divergent, and strange can find a connection to Mishka and its culture. Mishka is engineered to destroy everything boring and the mundane. Join the movement and reject normalcy." Theo's hair was still suffering from the rainbow tie-dye spiral coloring job he had convinced a nearby hairdresser to try on him a couple of weeks earlier.

He picked up his crutch and walked out of the room. Jorja and I followed. Stopping at the nurse's station, he said, "Hey, I'm outta my room. I'm walking out, as per my goal. Thanks guys. See ya later." He looked around the common area briefly and turned to walk to the elevator, using his crutch more as an ornament than an aid. One of the nurses called out to thank him for the delicious croissants he had given them from Trompeau's, his favorite French bakery. "Which one did you eat?" he asked.

"The sour cream," she said.

"Nice," he replied. "That's one of my favorites." The elevator doors closed. On the lower level, he paused while rounding the corner, a little unsure of his step, as a woman passed in the hallway. Through the sliding doors onto the driveway, he stopped by the car door and turned back toward the building. "Bye, Craig!" he said. I put the crutch in the trunk. We drove away.

The event was surprisingly low-key, reminiscent of the day Theo first walked between the parallel bars in the therapy gym. No fanfare, no parade of patients and doctors coming to say goodbye, no certificates of achievement or gold stars. Only a blast of congratulatory emails and text messages from friends who had heard the news, eliciting a post from him on Facebook: "Never have so many people congratulated me on discharging."

Theo had refused the most likely scenario Dr. Clifford had predicted for him the night of September 17, choosing to set his sights on a different outcome. I cannot possibly be qualified to second-guess Tim Bowers's choice. His injury was even more severe than Theo's. I have no idea what circumstances influenced his decision, but I admired the courage of his family for supporting him to make it. I could not help wondering, though, what he might have decided if he had first had the chance to spend fifteen minutes talking with Theo. He might have still made the same decision. Neither Tim nor Theo nor anyone else, can know with certainty the consequence of a decision in advance, nor can anyone ever know the outcome of the path not taken. A level of faith is always required, regardless of its origin, that the choice one makes is better than the choice not made.

I did not know that the choice about Theo's life was yet to be settled. For the moment, I was focused on the next step of his rehabilitation. Theo planned to stay in Denver to continue outpatient treatment at Craig. He would not be able to live on his own yet, so Jorja and I secured a short-term lease on a nearby apartment a couple of weeks before his discharge with a range of accessibility features the hospital recommended, including wheelchair access. A wheelchair never entered the front door, and none of the other features, like levered sink and door handles, were needed. Our biggest concerns, at first, were whether he would burn himself on the stove or a hot pan with no sensation of hot and cold on his right side or he would slip and fall while getting in and out of the shower with slow reflexes and limited strength.

To furnish the apartment, Jorja rented a basic set of furniture, including beds, a couch, and a dining room table. She went to the Goodwill store and bought about everything needed to outfit a kitchen. The "apartment beige" walls and carpeting were easy to match. Between Target and a couple of secondhand stores, she decorated the place with a few knickknacks, a fake plant, a couple of lamps, and a picture or two to ornament the walls. There was even an attractive, welcoming fall wreath on the outside of the front door. The hard work she put in to make the apartment as much like home as possible made a difference.

The Care Flite rescue scene just after the
Western Mountain Rescue team loaded Theo onto the helicopter

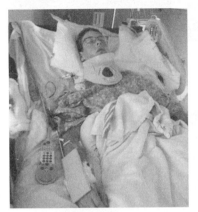

Theo, the day after surgery,
in St. Mary's Hospital ICU

Farid Tabaian, the first person
to find Theo on the trail

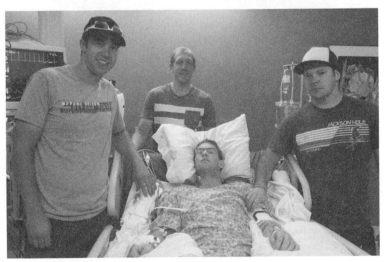

Left to Right: Eric Sjoreen, Scott Everhart, and Dan Miller
with Theo in the St. Mary's ICU

Left to Right: Carin Piazza, Michèle
Allgaier, Christine Landolt, and Irene
Rüesch, The four Swiss German women
who stayed with Theo on the mountain

Mae, Jorja, Theo, and Tim in the
gardens outside Craig Hospital

Meghan Cahill and Philip Cherry having lunch
with Theo on the patio at Craig Hospital

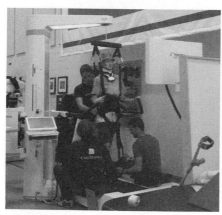

The Craig Hospital staff working with Theo
on the Locomat in the Peak Gymnasium

Chuck Hammond taking Theo
for his first walk outdoors

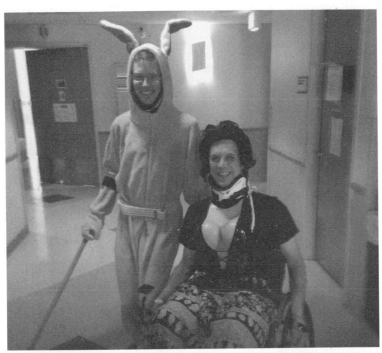

Theo and Jon Atwater make the rounds at Halloween

Maggie Ireland, Theo's outpatient physical therapist

Theo's first check up with Dr. Kirk Clifford, three months after walking out of Craig Hospital

Theo's first day back snowboarding at Vail

Theo's friend "Conrad" Ian McCarthy, who convinced him to try to snowboard again

Theo and Ashley Solze, the groom's sister, win the "Sexy Dance" at Mae's wedding

Jorja looks out at the horizon before tossing her bracelet into the sea in Cancun, Mexico

My contribution was to buy a cheap flat-screen TV and get cable TV and Internet installed. The day Theo was discharged and moved in, Jorja had stocked his new closet with favorite clothes from his closet in Vail. Fresh sheets were on the bed. His bathroom smelled of clean lemon Pine-Sol, and a new towel and washcloth hung on the rack.

It was not quite home. My Swiss coffee machine was in Dallas. Jorja's writing desk looking out over her "secret garden" was in Dallas. My bed was in Dallas. Theo was separated from the constant support of the hospital staff, but he was living with his parents for the first time in six years. Everything he cared about was a hundred-mile drive away, up in the mountains— it might as well have been a thousand miles. His snowboard gathered dust in the closet as the mountain was blanketed in snow. Nothing about our living situation was normal, and we all would rather have been home. For now, we were stuck in between.

Jorja and I have moved many times during our thirty years of marriage, always with a sense of excitement as we anticipated a new city, a bigger house, or a nicer neighborhood. None of that emotion happened to us in this move. Only a sense of duty provided the motivation for this move. Everything was temporary. The picture would be stuck to the wall, not nailed. The kitchenware would be given back to Goodwill or sold back to the secondhand store for pennies on the dollar. We installed disposable, stick-on window shades in the bedrooms, trimmed to size with scissors.

Jorja worked to establish a routine, shuttling Theo back and forth to therapy most days. She also began exercising regularly in the apartment complex gym in solidarity with Theo. I was working as much as I could stand, shuttling back and forth between Dallas and Denver. Even home did not feel like home. It was deafeningly quiet, the silence broken only by the cadence of the "tick-tock" from the old German wall clock I inherited from Mom and Dad and the occasional, melancholy chiming of the hour echoing through the house. When I was home, I wanted to be in Denver. When I was in Denver, I wanted to be home.

We "celebrated" Thanksgiving in the apartment. Celebration was not about the place, though, but about family, so we set aside the circumstances for the moment and looked forward to the festivity. Mae had moved into a drafty, seaside rental house in Plymouth, Massachusetts. She would pass by the site of the first recorded Thanksgiving dinner of 1621 along the drive to Boston Logan and would fly nearly 2,000 miles to spend the holiday with us in Denver.

I wrote about anticipating the day to friends and colleagues:

> As a family, we have eaten some of the best food the world has to offer in some of the most exciting places on the planet. Easily, the most important set of memories I carry are from meals we've shared together during our travels. But I can tell you with certainty that none of these remotely compare to the circumstances surrounding Thanksgiving in Denver.
>
> For a miraculous moment, we will all be there again, a perfect four. The view will be most spectacular. I think the turkey will be juicier than usual. The life-sustaining power of zwieback bread, the generations-old Krause version of manna, will be celebrated. Having suffered together as a family to this moment, we know each other differently and more deeply. We

know also that, behind our four, are hundreds of you who have fought for us, cried with us, prayed for us, and celebrated each bit of good news along the way.

The Thanksgiving holiday offered a brief, welcome departure from the routine. With a familiar "obstinate determination," Jorja managed to bake a turkey and prepare all our favorite side dishes, essentially on her own in an unfamiliar kitchen. To me, it appeared she did the whole thing using a mixing bowl, a wooden spoon, and a serrated paring knife. The day was wonderful, and then over. Mae flew back to the east coast to get back to work. We went back to work helping Theo get back to work.

Each day, one of us would drop Theo off at the hospital and pick him up after his sessions were finished. When he came back, we would want to know what he did and how it went. Some days, he was communicative and happy with the results. Other days were not so great. If Coni, his girlfriend, was there, we did our best to stay out of the way, to make excuses to leave for a while to give them some space.

We went out to eat most evenings. I lost twenty pounds during the two weeks Theo was in intensive care in Grand Junction, but I gained it all back—and then some—when we were living in the apartment. Theo likes ice cream. We ate a lot of ice cream. We walked to Whole Foods to get his hippie food, but we also went to King Sooper for tubs of Blue Bell Ice Cream. He also likes beer. We drank quite a bit of that, too. He was having difficulty putting on muscle mass, but I was very successful at putting on body mass. Occasionally we went to a show at the theater next door.

One evening, we dropped Theo off in Denver to spend time with a friend from college, and Jorja and I went to dinner.

He called to ask us to pick him up early because he was not feeling very well. By the time we pulled into the garage at the apartment building, he was shaking. Between the car and the front door of the apartment, his ability to walk deteriorated so quickly we had to stabilize him by holding his arm. We helped him into bed, and he began shaking uncontrollably. We had read material the hospital gave us in Theo's discharge papers about recognizing symptoms of autonomic dysreflexia, a very dangerous response SCI patients can have to infection or injury their bodies cannot feel. High blood pressure, nausea, pounding headache, a flushed face, and sweating are all signs. Jorja called the hospital.

The nurse suggested we treat it as though it were the flu and watch him carefully. We loaded him up with some Theraflu, which seemed to knock down the fever a little. The tension of fear drained slowly from Theo's face, and he drifted off to sleep. Jorja set an alarm to check on him at 2:00 a.m. He was still asleep. By morning, he was normal. Apparently, he had contracted some sort of twenty-four-hour flu bug, which passed quickly.

Theo's move to outpatient treatment was monumental. He was now away from the hospital, and there was no support infrastructure from his care team. He was now living on his own. He got himself to the hospital for rehab activities, and nobody provided a daily schedule stuck to a bulletin board.

Away from the constant encouragement of the hospital staff, Theo was struggling with self-motivation. Improvements were coming more slowly now, and none of them were headliners like "I walked today for the first time" or "I went up three flights of stairs." We would help him with his stretching exercises, especially getting his left arm moving with range of motion. When he relaxed on the couch or went to bed, he strapped a board to his hand designed to keep his fingers stretched flat, preventing the tendons from tightening. We attached an electronic stimulator to his arm and shoulder, which forced them to flex and to remind his brain where to find the muscles. With every inch of snowfall, and as last years' clients started to call Theo to schedule lessons for their upcoming trips, he became a little more frustrated.

W. H. Auden said, "The Time Being is, in a sense, the most trying time of all." We could sense Theo's mood darkening as the days passed. We all were tired, though. We all wanted to be in our respective homes. We still got up in the morning and tried to figure out ways to make the best of it. Theo did also, but the gap between what he promoted on the outside and how he was feeling on the inside grew. He wrote in his journal on December 4, "I'm sitting here on my bed, and I've just read two of the nicest, most seemingly genuine notes I've ever received. All I'm thinking is, 'Geeze. These people think I have been to Hell and back. I feel like a big phony. . . . Am I masquerading as something I am not?'" Beneath the entry, he sketched a picture of Charlie Brown's pitiful, wilted Christmas tree, bending almost double from the weight of a single ornament.

Maggie Ireland, Theo's outpatient physical therapist, was a bright spot. I met her for the first time when I brought him to one of his appointments. Maggie, in her late twenties, was strikingly beautiful. She was tall, almost six feet, and slender but not skinny—rather, more athletic. Her light brunette hair was pulled back neatly in a ponytail for work, and her hazel eyes were arched over by strong eyebrows, the kind made famous by Brooke Shields during her modeling days. She was dressed stylishly, but casually, as though she was headed out to meet good friends for Saturday brunch. Theo was not blind to Maggie's presence, but her outward beauty was not what motivated him into working with her.

One day, I hung around because the session with Maggie was the only one on his schedule for the morning. She became so deeply involved in the workout that both were winded by the end of the forty-five-minute session. This was what motivated Theo most. He wanted to squeeze every ounce of progress from each session, and he loved to work hard. She was a master of her craft. She knew exactly how far to push him, with a wary eye to any signs that the workout was going too far and that he was becoming frustrated. The session was efficient and well planned, moving logically through various muscle groups to maximize the result, pausing occasionally, but briefly, for Theo to catch his breath and take a few sips of water. She had discovered he wanted to work, but there was a limit. Her goal was to keep him in a positive mental state while still asking him to work beyond his own expectations but without allowing him to fall into frustration.

A hallmark of the Craig Hospital approach to therapy is a willingness to adapt treatment to fit the unique needs of the patient. Theo had taken to calling her "Maggie of Ireland," and one afternoon, as they were brainstorming the best way to help with his agility, Theo mustered his best Irish accent and, half-joking, asked, "Maggie of Ireland, will ya teach me an Irish jig?" She agreed, and, each week, she would teach him a new segment of the jig. At first, he struggled, clumsily stumbling as he worked to throw his feet into the right position, crossing one leg in front of the other, touching his toe to the ground behind. But each week saw improvement as he quickly gained a new awareness of how he could control his changed body. The Irish jig was a perfect exercise.

The far-reaching impact of Maggie's work, as well as that of her colleagues, was on full display as Craig Hospital held its annual Christmas program in the Peak Gymnasium. All the high-tech equipment had been pushed aside to make room for choir rafters, an electronic piano, microphones, and folding chairs. Theo debated whether he wanted to go because he felt self-conscious about walking into the gym in front of all those people who would never walk again. But he decided to go, if only to show support for a few of the key people who had cared for him and would be "performing."

While the room filled with patients, family, friends, and hospital staff, the lively buzz of conversation grew, and one could sense that the Peak Gymnasium was being transformed in anticipation of a completely different dimension of therapy. Theo and I stepped around wheelchairs, walkers, and hospital beds to our seats in the back row, off to one side in the reserved patient/family section as if to say, "We only sort of belong here." By looking at us, you might have wondered if we were out of place and should be in the back with the rest of the crowd, sort of the way you look at someone who you think did not have the right to park in that handicapped space next to the front door.

Theo did not look like a patient. He walked down the steps and across to the far side of the gym. His neck brace was gone, his crutch was gone, and his gait was steady. Unless someone looked closely to see the four-inch scar down the back of his neck or that his left arm and hand were still struggling to catch up, hidden beneath his jacket sleeve, no one would have thought he belonged here. Theo refers to his scar as the "Yale scar" because it is perfectly centered and vertically straight from the incision created by the Yale-trained surgeon in Grand Junction.

By the time of the Christmas party, we had already agreed with Theo that he would move back to Vail on New Year's Day.

The master of ceremonies, one of the doctors, stopped short of the customary greeting, "We are glad you are here." He acknowledged that most who were there, including those who were watching the program from their rooms on closed-circuit TV, were not expecting Peak Gymnasium to be the place they spent their Christmas holiday. As long as they were there, they would celebrate together the hope for healing that would come from partnership between caregiver and patient.

This partnership framed in hope was the point of the program. We were all there anticipating the coming of something more. The program unfolded with a mélange of sing-along carols, a rap song from a doctor, poetry from a night technician, a men's quartet, and a full choir. The occasional interruption from a timer reminding some patients to shift their weight in their wheelchairs to avoid pressure sores was as normal as the sound of jingling bells. Not a single performance on this night would have made it to the American Idol auditions I had been watching so intently the night of September 17. The production was masterful just the same, with a singular focus on what counted: we were here together now, so let us celebrate the hope of healing and the better life that is to come.

The "peak," for me, happened when Rex marched up to the microphone as the final act. Rex, who had been a local Denver radio personality through his late-night show, served food in the Craig Hospital cafeteria because he wanted to. In the program, Rex entered the gym with a dramatic flair, wearing a black suit and sunglasses as the PA boomed the introduction: "Professor Tony, the Professor of Inspiration from the University of Lost Minds." If you wanted to be inspired, he said, you only needed to look around the room where the magic of human inspiration between staff and patient was on display. If all you could do was smile, then you should smile, hold nothing back, because even a smile is a sign of personal, inner healing.

The songs had been sung, and Santa made his appearance preceded by eight therapy dogs wearing fuzzy antlers. The smiles on faces across the gym as the program closed with the singing of "We Wish You a Merry Christmas" were a clear measure that this therapy session had its intended effect, and just a little more healing had come.

We went to the Christmas Eve service at Calvary Baptist Church of Denver, not more than a quarter of a mile down the road. In another odd twist of coincidence, we knew both pastors extremely well. Senior Pastor Anne Jernberg Scalfaro had grown up in our church, and her parents had been Theo's and Mae's first grade Sunday school teachers. Both Anne and Executive Pastor Andrew Daugherty spent two years at our church back in Dallas in a postseminary residency program.

We did our best to celebrate Christmas Day at the apartment, but it was far from normal. I projected a FaceTime video with Mae onto the TV so we could sort of open gifts together. We enjoyed watching each other open presents and visited a little, but by 10:00 a.m., we were trying to figure out how we would pass the rest of the day.

Four years earlier, our family was sitting around our living room in the Paris suburbs trying to figure out the same thing. By noon, we were in the car, driving to Germany. We still remember that as one of the most fun Christmases ever. This time, though, the stress of the last three months, the abnormal living circumstances, and the looming prospect that the day was coming for us to let go of Theo once more weighed heavily on everyone.

We learned to give Theo a certain amount of space and quiet he has needed since middle school. The last few weeks of December in Colorado were no different. What we did not know was the darkness of his despair. He wrote in his journal on Christmas Day: "I should be happy, but today I really really want to end my own life. I am filled with an indescribable amount of self-loathing and a general desire to hurt others. I wish I could crush the spirit of my mother to the point that she is crying for days and starts to feel the same hatred I feel for myself. I wonder if I have the strength in my legs to jump out the window and crack my skull and do what that fucking aspen tree should have done three months ago."

The next day, though, he got out of bed, showered, and packed, without divulging a hint of these thoughts. The three of us went to the airport and checked in to fly to Boston to spend a few days with Mae. We did not need wheelchair assistance, we did not need extra time for boarding, and we could have said "yes" to whether we were willing and able to assist in case of emergency had we been seated in the exit row. We were not seated in the exit row, though, because I had cashed in first class upgrades.

12

Jorja

From his earliest days I enjoyed that our Theo had the same first name as one of my favorite American presidents, Theodore Roosevelt, who embraced a strenuous lifestyle to overcome childhood frailty and to later became known for his exuberant personality and his robust physical fitness. Theo embraced robust physical exertion and fitness as a lifestyle more and more as he grew up.

Now, Theo's disaster on the mountain had added a new, but unwelcome, parallel: a terrible struggle to surmount debilitating, life-threatening infirmity. Theo's approach to rehabilitation mirrored Roosevelt's words: "It is only through labor and painful effort, by grim energy and resolute courage, that we move on to better things." The dogged effort Theo exhibited in the therapy kitchen disaster also echoed how Jorja transformed our sparse apartment into a home and, by force of her unyielding will, to bring about Thanksgiving dinner.

This was the resolute determination Theo exhibited throughout his rehab at Craig, the "spirit of my mother" he so desperately wanted to crush in his raging journal entry. As the workmanlike days of rehabilitation ground along, I began to awaken to a reality that has since become very precious.

Through this whole experience, Jorja was, in many respects, an omnipresent spirit moving behind the scenes. While I was crying, or writing updates, or screaming at insurance agents, she was quietly and steadily keeping vigil, praying, and working. She wept privately, drawing strength from Scripture and poetry she read in quiet times. She showed up with strength in front of Theo, Mae, and me. From the moment we stepped off the plane in Grand Junction on September 18, she was dedicated to a single purpose: Theo's recovery.

Jorja carried a prayer from *Gitanjali,* a book of poems by Rabindranath Tagore, with her throughout Theo's recovery called "The Grasp of Your Hand":

> Let me not pray to be sheltered from dangers, but to be fearless in facing them.
>
> Let me not beg for the stilling of my pain, but for the heart to conquer it.
>
> Let me not crave in anxious fear to be saved, but hope for the patience to win my freedom.
>
> Grant me that I may not be a coward, feeling Your mercy in my success alone; but let me find the grasp of Your hand in my failures.

This prayer has been the theme of her life. Her very name, with its unusual spelling, is an ever-present reminder of her origin in suffering and grace that formed in her a character of tender love and steel.

Jorja is adopted. She was taken by the state from her aunt's home at age five when a concerned neighbor called Child Protective Services. She had bad teeth, one small bag of toys, and the clothes she was wearing that day. And she was being sexually abused by her uncle and another man who she assumed was his friend, an abuse which she also assumed was normal, something all kids did.

Then she arrived at Dean and Betty Morton's house.

Dean and Betty Morton had no biological children, but they fostered more than a hundred children through the years and adopted five, one of whom was Jorja. When the adoption was finalized, she was given a chance to change her name to anything she wanted. Older sister Leslie helped her arrive at "Jorja," which was a truncated version of her original name, "Georgetta." "Jorja" was shorter and much easier to spell on school papers.

To say her adoptive parents were not wealthy is like saying Lichtenstein is not a big country. When they were married, their first home was a converted smoke house on Betty's sister's farm with an attached chicken coop. A truck bed served as the porch. It may have been the original "tiny house." At some point, they scraped together enough money to buy a small nineteenth-century farm house on the outskirts of Sedalia, Missouri, where Jorja was deposited as a little girl. Dean worked in highway construction most of his life and was usually gone except on the weekend. Betty worked part time in the juvenile detention center to help make ends meet, but she mostly managed the household and ran the revolving door of kids coming in and going out. Jorja was always excited to see who might be there when she came home from school on any given day.

One summer, Dean and Betty also agreed to house a college-aged summer missionary named June DeWitt, who was working at their church. June took a special interest in Jorja and started teaching her to sing. Jorja remembers practicing while standing on a stump out in the backyard of their home, singing at the top of her lungs:

I sing because I'm happy,
I sing because I'm free,
For His eye is on the sparrow,
And I know He watches me.

June secretly funded a scholarship to help Jorja attend William Jewell College, where she majored in music education and vocal performance. June, now retired from a long career as an elementary music teacher, became a lifelong mentor to Jorja.

I met Jorja at William Jewell. Although I was headed down a track to major in physics, I spent a lot of time in the music building, playing in the orchestra and jazz band and taking trumpet lessons. I saw her one day as she was briskly crossing the street to the music building, wearing a bright blue-and-yellow coat. Her big smile scrunched her cheeks, making narrow slits, behind which one could just see those intense blue-green eyes. It was a physics major's dream. I told my roommate, "I'm going to marry her." He said I did not have a chance. I did, as it turned out, but I had to join a choir to get close enough.

The distance between Jorja's heart and her lips is as short as any I've ever experienced, only challenged by the speed with which she also can catapult herself from abject despair to euphoric joy. I never saw anyone who could feel so much, and that is mostly good for someone like me, who lives emotionally in the deep and with little variance. It can also be challenging, but I could not tear my eyes away. We were married just after college, almost thirty-five years ago.

Jorja operates at only two speeds, I tell people: at a full sprint or fast asleep. It is a good thing that she is always near her bed when she falls asleep; otherwise, she would get hurt. Moderation is an alien concept. She brought her childhood experience and this philosophy tenaciously into our family. She carried the same ferocity into the classroom where she taught music and applies it today as she volunteers at a nonprofit safe haven called Our Friends Place dedicated to ending the cycle of poverty for troubled or abused girls ages eighteen to twenty-four.

Theo's trauma had so deeply injured her also because she spent every waking moment of his and Mac's formative years loving, disciplining, and otherwise protecting them from every harm. This harm was one she could not fix for him.

What she could do was give him the tools to face it himself. Theo's resolute determination, his inability to dedicate anything less than everything in a task, and his ability to catapult himself out of despair were all gifts from Jorja. She may not admit it as such, and I am embarrassed to say I did not see the connection until Theo's injury happened, but they were plain for everyone to see.

Theo is his mother's son.

13

A Long Way from Home

We drove Theo to Vail on New Year's Eve Day. The car trunk was packed with everything he brought into Craig Hospital but with almost nothing he was given while there—no wheelchair, no walker, no crutch. Theo's crutch was now replaced by a cane we found at a secondhand store. We bought it for the metal spike attached to the end he could flip down to provide traction in ice and snow. Theo was ready to be home, and we were ready to be home. Dropping him off and leaving, though, was gut-wrenching, reminiscent of the day we left him behind to begin his freshman year at Denver University, only much worse.

The two-hour drive into the mountains was quiet. We were tired, stressed, excited, and afraid. Jorja and I did not hang around after unloading Theo's belongings into his room in Vail. Nothing was left to do, and a prolonged goodbye would be unbearable. A renovation of Theo's bathroom we started a month before he was hurt had just been completed. After the accident, I made sure the contractor used faucets with levers in case Theo could not grip a knob, but he could. I also arranged to have heavy bannisters installed along all the stairs, from the parking lot to the front door, and then indoors from the first floor to the second. I never saw him touch them. His neighbor, Mike, agreed to make sure snow was shoveled and ice was chipped away from the path to Theo's car through the winter. His clothes were put away in the closet. It was time for us to go.

Meg Cahill was there when we left and remembers it well. "I knew it was hard for you," she told me. "You had just been with him through one of the hardest processes ever, and you were sending him off. Jorja seemed strong about leaving, but you were really upset." Theo was in a different place. After we left, Meg asked him how he was, and he said, "I'm fine. I'm so ready for a break from living with them." Jorja and I knew that, of course. The stress had been building for several weeks. Theo wanted just to be on his couch, listening to music, or in his kitchen, cooking some food the way he liked. That he was physically able to cook for himself was cause for joy, but Jorja and I could see only menacing hot burners he could not feel and dangerous sharp knives, now awkward to handle. Life was heavy.

In contrast, everyone around us cheered. Doctors, his friends, and our friends saw only an inspiring, miraculous victory. "He's young. He'll be fine," they said. "Isn't he right-handed? Thank God it isn't his right hand." By any measure, we had miraculously met our goal. He was walking. He could take care of himself. He could even dance an Irish jig. He was living on his own, back in his home. He would start back to work the next week, both at the Ritz and at the ski school.

I went first, wrapping Theo in a big bear hug, holding him tightly. He reciprocated, although his left arm trembled slightly as he strained to hold it close across my back. I could feel the pit just below his left shoulder blade vacated by a disconnected muscle. I held on a long time, desperate to store every detail of the sensation in my memory. I could not produce any words, looking away as I let go and stepped back. Jorja held her composure as she reached through his arms, up to his shoulders and kissed him lightly on the cheek. "We love you so much," she said softly, for both of us. She lingered. I waited, staring at the floor. When she finally let go, we turned away, closed the front door behind us, and rushed to the car.

We drove away in tears, both of us. Jorja's wall crumbled before we made it out of the parking lot. She cried the same, deep cry only a mother can cry, as she did the night of the accident. I grabbed Jorja's hand as I peered through my clouded eyes, my left hand tightly gripping the steering wheel to follow the twists of I-70 through the East Vail canyon, up across Vail Pass. Jorja's fingernails dug into the palm of my hand as she braced against the pain flooding her soul.

Even Colorado was estranged from us, by its very nature having been the main instigator of our tragedy. It had betrayed us. Deep snow smothered the landscape and weighed heavily on the evergreen trees alongside the highway. Normally we would admire the beauty. Today we saw a heavy burden. The champagne powder snow was a cold hazard to be avoided rather than an inviting canvas to carve through on freshly waxed skis.

We were silent through Silverthorne, past the turnoff to Breckenridge, where our family skied the second year together, through the Eisenhower Tunnel, and past Idaho Springs, where Theo had introduced our family to Beau Jo's Pizza a few years ago. The snow was gone by the time we made the final descent out of the foothills past Boulder into Denver. The silence was now broken only by conversation about how we would most efficiently break camp at the apartment to leave for Dallas.

Back in Denver, we tried to focus on the short-term task in front of us. We ate because it was time to eat, not because we were hungry. The food was bland. The rental furniture was picked up. We left about everything else at the back door of the Goodwill store. We packed our bags, dropped the keys at the leasing office, and drove away. I have never become particularly attached to any place we have lived. That apartment was dead to me.

After 108 days, we were done. I drew in one last glimpse of Mount Evans and the Colorado Rockies in the distance until the left-turn light turned green. We turned southeast toward home with our car and our hearts loaded to the brim. The landscape empathized, while the defiant peaks of Colorado, now barricading us from access to what we cherished most, yielded to the blunt mesas of northern New Mexico and the numbing plains of west Texas, coaxing us to let go and push ahead to home. By the time we descended the cap rock in that vast expanse of "in between" from Amarillo to Wichita Falls, we just wanted to be home.

My mind drifted in the monotony of the dashed centerline disappearing with a steady pulse under the car, splitting an endless landscape of mesquite trees and idle oil well pumps. The repeating pattern of people coming in and out of our lives, especially Theo's life, at just the right time, and with just the right experience, haunted me again. The people we encountered at Craig were uniquely and specifically equipped. How did they get to us at that most critical time in our lives?

"I found rehab through the grace of God," Dr. Berliner told me. The perspective was striking from a man who basically found his career through losing his eye to cancer at age eleven. His mother, a pharmaceutical sales rep, was always a forceful influence on his life. One day, she was watching him play soccer and noticed an unusual bulge around his eye. She took him off the field to a doctor and demanded an MRI. This technology was new at the time and turned up negative results the first time, but Jeff's skeptical mother demanded a second test. The second showed a tumor growing behind his left eye.

Jeff attributes Dr. David Abramson at New York Hospital with saving his life in more ways than one. Dr. Abramson successfully removed the tumor, and through two more years of grueling chemotherapy and radiation, the cancer was stopped. Along the way, the doctor became a mentor and friend to Jeff. One afternoon Dr. Abramson took Jeff to a New York Jets football game and pulled him aside between quarters to say, "Jeff, you are going to be a doctor one day. Always remember to help people in need."

Jeff never wanted to return to any hospital, though, especially one having anything to do with cancer treatment. He tried almost every other career path, from waiting tables to being a stock broker, finally settling on becoming a school teacher, until the day his high school principal told him, "Jeff, you are a fine teacher, but I see you more as a doctor."

Unable to escape Dr. Abramson's prophetic words, he left teaching for medical school and was hired at Craig the same year as Theo's accident, seven years after a fellowship at Baylor College of Medicine in Houston, Texas, introduced him to spinal cord injury rehabilitation focused on cancer patients. He enjoyed internal medicine and neurology but most loved the aspect of functionally helping the patient. "You get to take them through the toughest times of their lives," he said. "Everyone remembers their first rehab doctor. You become a part of their lives, and that's what I love."

Dr. B engaged Theo on a peer-to-peer basis, lingering more than any other doctor during his visits. He obviously craved the engagement with his patient, figuring out together how to coax another element of functional improvement from the body. No detail was too small, no subject off limits. As Theo transitioned from being confined to the bed and the wheelchair, Dr. B coached him that he should begin to exercise his bladder control muscles because the catheter would be coming out soon. The control nerves for bowel and bladder are particularly sensitive and might not work even if he regained his mobility.

The two also broached the touchy subject of sexual function. Dr. B explained that it was time to be "practicing." Theo was thrilled and relieved the day he called me to pronounce, "Dad, don't tell Mom, but I was able to get the soldiers out of the barracks today!"

Dr. B found his way to his vocation through a tragic illness and the powerful influence of a mentor who saw his potential. Theo said of Dr. B, "He was the first person who really understood me and what I was dealing with. My perception was that he came in with new thoughts and ideas for my situation."

Much like Dr. B, Chuck Hammond, Theo's physical therapist, was also headed down a path to become a school teacher. His mother was a teacher. Chuck entered the University of Northern Colorado without thinking too much about what he wanted to be. He "floundered around a little," but he ultimately decided to pursue teaching. In his final year during his student teaching assignment, he lost confidence in the decision because standing in front of a large class was intimidating. Low on money, he finished his degree and certification anyway, taking a job across the street from Craig Hospital at Swedish Hospital to help pay the bills. A year later, Chuck told his wife, "This has me written all over it." In the one-on-one setting of physical therapy, he discovered he could be more effective, being responsible for outcomes in partnership with the patient, the patient's family, and the rest of the care team.

He was accepted into the highly competitive physical therapy program at the University of Colorado, and fifteen months later, with a new baby and with a degree in hand, he was hired as a physical therapist at Craig Hospital. He considers those fifteen months one of the toughest periods of his life, but he knows about goals, about the discipline required to reach them. He radiates a cool confidence in the way he works with patients. Chuck is a teacher, for sure, but he is a person-to-person teacher, more like a tutor. He revels in the idea of solving the puzzle, learning exactly what motivates and what frustrates a person. He looks for ways to establish a goal that he knows is achievable but that is just beyond where the patient believes he or she is capable.

The cocktail of Chuck Hammond is part teacher, part physical therapist, and part psychologist. Stirred with the positive inspiration he channels from his family and seasoned with his own life experience, it was the perfect elixir for Theo's progress. The common philosophy he shares with Theo on the importance of setting and meeting goals with personal accountability translated to astonishing results. Chuck was consistently able to unlock Theo's spirit of determination and drive.

For Chuck's colleague, Caitlin Glennon, all was proceeding according to plan, through the kinesiology degree at Arizona State and the master's at University of Wisconsin, until the original clinic she was assigned to for two months of field work was unable to accommodate her. Her program coordinator redirected her to a hospital that specialized in spinal injuries. After working there three months, she was hooked and immediately began to look for a full-time position.

"Craig Hospital," she said, "was one of the few places you could go and just do what is right for patients. The place was patient centered, and you were never going to talk about units or funding for equipment. It was all about the patient." Unsuccessful with her first application, she returned to school for another year and then reapplied. She had been at Craig for three years when she became Theo's OT.

The perspective Caitlin brought to Theo's recovery, instilled in her from an early age, was that he was already normal. As they discussed every aspect of daily living, solving potential problems, his self-confidence grew. They could discuss anything. One conversation she will never forget had a reverse effect. Theo was discussing a possible treatment with Dr. B involving targeted Botox injections to help balance muscle function. Caitlin was explaining the therapeutic use to him. The conversation somehow moved to women's use of Botox as a beauty treatment.

This was something Theo was quite familiar with, having grown up in and around Dallas, Texas, where the treatment is widely used. He said, "It just doesn't look natural. It's like their face doesn't move." Drawing an analogy between the miles an automobile travels and the age of a person, he shook his head as he looked at her and said, "I just don't get women, sometimes. Miles are sexy. Wrinkles are sexy. It says where you've been and what you've learned." Caitlin was pregnant at the time and experiencing all the changes to her body as it prepared itself for motherhood. "That was a telltale moment for me, too," she told me. "It showed me how deep he was for his age. He was saying experience and knowledge are so much more attractive than the perfect face." She thinks about it almost every morning when she wakes up and looks in the mirror. "Okay. Miles are sexy."

Maggie Ireland was crowned Miss Colorado in 2007. Her path to becoming Theo's outpatient physical therapist is perhaps the most extraordinary story of all. I watched with millions of other Americans on April 20, 1999, as the Columbine High School massacre unfolded in Littleton, Colorado. The shocking video of an injured student climbing out the window of the building aided by SWAT team members was played on networks around the clock and featured on CNN's twenty-fifth anniversary show "Twenty-Five Stories that Touched our Lives" in 2009.

The student hanging from the window, then known only as "the boy in the window," was Patrick Ireland, Maggie's older brother. Shot twice in the head, the right side of his body paralyzed, it took him three-and-a-half hours to crawl to the window and get the attention of the authorities. After emergency surgery and ten days in St. Anthony's Hospital in Denver, Patrick was transferred to Craig Hospital for rehabilitation.

Many days, Maggie was sitting by his bedside at Craig Hospital watching the doctors, nurses, and therapists shuttle in and out for his care. After Patrick was discharged, Maggie decided to join her mother as a volunteer at Craig on the weekends. Entering high school, she decided she wanted to be a physical therapist, and she wanted to spend her career at Craig Hospital. The year Theo was injured was her first year at Craig Hospital.

In a 2008 interview with *Access Hollywood*, Maggie told the story of her brother's accident and concluded, "I want to work with survivors of brain and spinal cord injury at Craig Hospital and just make that impact on not only the patients but also the families like ours whose lives have been impacted." She was in Las Vegas at the time of the interview, preparing for the Miss America pageant.

Her talent for the competition, as it turns out, was performing an Irish step dance. In the *Las Vegas Review Journal*, Norm Clarke reported, "Miss Colorado, Maggie Ireland, the tallest competitor at 5'11", dazzled with her agility while performing an Irish step dance version of 'Footloose.'" Her platform for the competition was titled "Opening the Door to Optimism," and her message was that some type of good can come out of any situation. Because she did not readily advertise this phase of her life, Theo did not know any of this when he asked her to teach him the jig.

Maggie knew firsthand what Theo had lost, how far he had to go, and what was ahead as he fought for his future. "Optimism is the key to life," Maggie told Bill Husted of the *Denver Post* in 2007 after winning the Miss Colorado beauty pageant. "Waking up with a positive attitude or changing your attitude through a life-changing event." She had dedicated herself to helping others through that battle for a future and was convinced that optimism was key to success. Beauty, to her, was to see something good happen out of a tragic loss.

The stories of Jeff Berliner, Chuck Hammond, Caitlin Glennon, Maggie Ireland, and even Jon Atwater and Charles Drahota expanded the confluence of strangers backwards in time, long before Theo torpedoed an aspen tree. Not only did they all happen to show up at the right time with peculiar gifts and experiences uniquely tailored to Theo's need, but also, for most, a life-changing event in each of their histories forced them to pursue options they otherwise never would have considered, opening the path leading to an intersection with Theo. These people attribute who they are to influence from a forceful parent or an influential mentor.

The formative influence of a parent is inescapable. Who I am is heavily influenced by my parents and their histories, as it is for my own children with me. I am unavoidably the son of a Baptist preacher and of a forceful, God-fearing mother. Theo, suddenly facing his mortality as he lay motionless on the mountain, was reminded of his mother's touch as Christine Landolt gently stroked his hair. Theo also refers to Christine as an "angel." From the first day of kindergarten, when young Teddy told his mother, "It'll be okay, Mom," to the dark words he scribbled across the pages of his journal on Christmas Day, Theo acknowledged the inescapable influence of his mother's resilient spirit in who he was to become.

If there was ever a case for the existence of God and the connected influence inherent in a world created by Him, the precedent case was sitting next to me in the car. A little girl was plucked from a dark corner of the world because a neighbor noticed and made a call. The consequence of that phone call, Dean and Betty's decision to provide a sanctuary, and a mentor's influence on her life path have impacted hundreds of kids who have caught a passion for music from her teaching, many of whom have gone on to do the same for others.

Theo was not only the beneficiary of his mother's strength, and not just of those who were stepping in just now, but also of people who came before, people he will never know. The cascading and connected impact of influencers who stepped up to play roles in critical moments in the histories of those who helped Theo as their lives intersected his was intimidating. Only the most narcissistic logic would conclude these people were guided through their lives for the express purpose of coming to the aid of my son in his moment of need.

Instead, on my way back to Dallas, to my friends, and to my colleagues, this pattern of helpers forced me to consider my own contribution. The world around us presents plenty of obstacles to distract and inhibit our chosen path. Yet these same obstacles, especially the big ones, can unearth dramatic discoveries about who we are, which, in turn, can have an extraordinary impact on others. Was I doing enough to help?

We pulled into the garage at home just before dusk. After unloading the car, I sat down to write an update to friends and colleagues: "We are each where we belong. Theo is living fully on his own in Vail, still pushing himself to get better. Mae is in Plymouth, experiencing her first beach blizzard. We are back in Dallas. Jorja is trying to remember where she put anything three months ago, and I am sitting at the computer, having first wound Dad's clock."

I inherited two things from my mom and dad I cherish most: Mom's breadbox—I see her every time I slide open the lid—and one of Dad's antique striking clocks he was given by a church in Germany. I wound it the morning of September 18, just before we rushed out the door, and from time to time as I stopped through Dallas. It had never stopped. Except, it was stopped on that January afternoon when we walked into the house. We had been gone too long. It seemed everyone was done, even the clock. I wound the clock and set the time. Now we could move on. We were all home.

14

"He's Back."

Theo's first day back to work began as prescribed. He set his alarm early to allow extra time. He cooked breakfast, having learned to check the temperature of the pan with his left hand, weak but with sensation, and then grab the handle with his right hand, strong but with no sensation of hot and cold. He showered and dressed, buttoning his shirt and tying his shoes, both arduous but doable tasks thanks to Caitlin's occupational therapy sessions. He decided to walk to the bus stop ten minutes away instead of driving his car to work because he could. Thanks to Chuck's early coaching, he easily navigated the seventeen steps from the top floor to the front door and seventeen more to the parking lot, never touching the beautifully hand-crafted bannisters I had the carpenter install. Theo swung around the corner at the landing, clear because the neighbor had spread chemical pellets to thaw the ice, as we had requested.

Turning down the driveway and onto the open street, Theo had picked up his pace about the time the right heel of his boot met a slippery patch of packed snow. His foot shot forward as his body ignored the response from his brain. Up both legs went into the air, where Newton's laws of motion took over, slamming him hard to the ground on his back. His neck snapped back, bouncing the back of his head off the snow-packed road. Dazed and aching, he lay motionless in the middle of the road, taking inventory of the damage, but he realized, "I didn't break my neck." He slowly gathered himself onto his knees and stood, dusted the snow from his coat, and walked on to the bus stop. "It was a liberating experience," he told me later. "I realized that I could fall, and I wouldn't break my neck. From then on, I wasn't going to be afraid, and I would try everything."

He received a hero's welcome his first day back at the ski school and his first day back at the Ritz. Scott Everhardt treated him like a celebrity, keeping him away from people. Eric Sjoreen, in charge of security at the Ritz and still punishing himself for not warning Theo about that curve in the trail, was thrilled to see him looking so normal. "I walked in, and he was shaking hands with everybody," Eric said, "just being his normal self as though nothing had happened."

Anyone seeing him for the first time since the accident was shocked by what he could do compared to the initial stories they had heard about his accident. It was incredible, they thought, what he had accomplished. Inspiring. Theo basically looked normal to most of his casual friends and colleagues because he had become skilled at masking his lingering physical deficits. Those who had seen him soon after his accident would say, "He looks amazing!" Or they would say, "He may not be 100 percent, but look how far he has come." They all meant well and rejoiced with him in his success so far.

They largely returned to their own sense of normalcy, assuming he was now out of danger and he no longer needed their heightened attention. From Theo's point of view, he was not out of danger. Frustrated by the many people who called or wrote or came to see him when he was in the hospital but who now had moved on, he felt isolated. Dan, Eric, and Scott had not forgotten, but they also did not discuss his injury unless Theo brought it up—which was never.

"Trying everything" included getting back on a snowboard if Theo wanted to return to his teaching job at the Vail ski school. He grudgingly started back to physical therapy two days a week at the local Howard Head Sports Rehabilitation Clinic, making slow progress but strengthening his core, his grip, and his agility. Until he felt strong enough to brave the ski slopes, he worked indoors at the ticket office, awkwardly typing on a keyboard and shuffling paper in front of anxious parents who were registering impatient children into ski school for the day.

Figuring out what to do with his life in a mountain town, where the falling snow served only as a constant reminder of what he could no longer do, was a frustrating, lonely job. Theo projected a happy façade in front of his friends, but there were more bad days than good. Occasionally his sense of humor peeked through, such as the day he had yet another fall in the fresh snow outside the ski school office. "After capturing the hearts of his surgery staff," Theo posted on Facebook, "we return to our hero, lying in the middle of the street, enveloped in a cloud of cold, white, and coincidentally, comfortable humility."

At the end of January, Theo was scheduled to see his surgeon, Dr. Clifford, for a three-month checkup. He would drive to Grand Junction for the first time since the accident, so Jorja flew up to accompany him to the appointment. They took advantage of the trip to visit the ICU at St. Mary's before going to Dr. Clifford's office. Theo had no memory of the ICU facility as he strolled the hallway, not even able to identify which room had been his for those eight days, but he recognized members of the staff who had helped him. Wide smiles broke across their faces in a rare opportunity to see the fruit of their work as they recalled the first days together, and Theo showed what he could now do, thanking each of them for the part they played. These were people who understood him and fully appreciated what was happening. His reception raised Theo's spirit.

Dr. Clifford already knew what Theo could do, having been in contact with Craig Hospital to keep up with his progress, but to see it was another thing altogether. Theo stood to greet him when Dr. Clifford entered the exam room and then seated himself on the exam table as Dr. Clifford sat in a chair across from him. They talked briefly about how Theo was feeling, and Dr. Clifford reported that Dr. Hsu had recently called him from Craig to say he had never seen anyone who presented with Theo's degree of neurologic compromise end up walking out of Craig.

"So let me see you walk!" he commanded. Theo, maybe for dramatic effect, slowly raised himself off the table with his arms and turned carefully toward the door. He paused briefly, as if to gain his balance, and abruptly began high stepping across the room. as if he were on parade in a marching band. "Ha*haaa*!" Dr. Clifford shouted. "That is absolutely amazing. I cannot believe that!" Theo, smiling broadly as if he had carried off a well-planned prank, spun and returned, plopping down on the exam table. Dr. Clifford checked the strength in Theo's hands and arms, admiring him as a master craftsman would study his freshly completed piece of furniture. "Theo, you're still going to see improvement," he said. Then, running his hand lightly across the scar on the back of Theo's neck, Dr. Clifford assured Theo, "That's going to fade over time."

Then Dr. Clifford sat down and paused a moment, staring at the floor to process what he had seen. He glanced at Jorja, returned his gaze to Theo, and finally, shaking his head, blurted out, "I talk about you all the time. You remember me telling you you would never walk again?"

"Yeah," Theo said. "My uncles and my aunt came to visit me in Craig. I told them the phrase "fuck that shit" instantly popped into my head when you said that to me." After a nervous chuckle, he added, "Pardon the French, but that was where my mind was. It's like when Neo just says no to the bullets."

"Yeah, that's about what you are," Dr. Clifford gushed. "You're like Matrix." He struggled to organize his thoughts into words. "Whatever you did, I wish we could replicate it. I never tell patients like you they're going to walk because they don't. You are literally one in a million. I wish I could take the credit. You are a miracle kid. I never thought there'd be any way you'd walk again."

Dr. Clifford's words echoed across the canyons as Theo drove back to Vail. His accident was a strange fluke, but his recovery was outlandish. Jorja and I celebrated the report. Maybe life was moving on after all. Theo, on the other hand, felt enormous pressure, trapped between the expectation of a miracle and the futility of a broken future.

He kept the pressure to himself, though, when our whole family convened back in Vail, including Mae's boyfriend Dale Solze, under the pretense we were going to ski and celebrate Mae's birthday. Dale proposed to Mae on the trip, finally relieving us of keeping the secret from the day he called Theo and me in October. Theo was lying in a hospital bed unable to feed himself, me sitting by his side, both of us fearing what might be our future. The silence between us had been broken by the "ding" of a text message arriving on my phone. Dale wanted to know if this was a good time to speak to both Theo and me. I told Theo, "Get ready. This can only mean one thing." When the phone rang, Dale had his speech ready.

Dale said he knew we were the two most important men in Mae's life and wondered if there was any reason we would be opposed to him asking Mae to marry him. As I scrambled to gather my composure, I shoved the phone over near Theo, mouthing silently, "You go first." Without hesitation, Theo said, "Dale, I have a tremendous amount of respect for you. I can't imagine a better fit for Mae, and I would be honored to have you as a brother." Taking Theo's cue, I mumbled some awkward joke about how his only character flaw was that he was an Ohio State Buckeye fan, but I essentially repeated the endorsement he received from Mae's brother.

The engagement was a concrete reminder to Jorja and me that life continues and good things could still happen. Unfortunately, good things were not happening the same way for Theo. As his mood darkened with the slowing rate of progress he was making physically, his girlfriend, Coni, was increasingly anxious about their future. Under pressure from her mother to come home, she booked a flight to Argentina in early April. Theo volunteered to drive her to the airport in Denver, where the issue came to a boil. The commitment she needed, he could not give. She wanted to know if he would be there for her if she decided to return. He was not sure he would be there at all. They were like two people who shared the intimate horror of fighting a war no one else could understand, but the security entrance at

Denver International Airport that day marked the end of their journey together. There was just too much baggage to carry on.

Theo returned his attention to the business of trying everything. He dropped physical therapy sessions, instead taking up a weekly yoga class in Breckenridge. He discovered that, by combining exercises from the two methods, he made faster progress. One day, while working the front drive at the Ritz, he happened to be in the garage at the same time as another valet who had just parked a car. Without thinking, he challenged his colleague to see who could reach the elevator first. He sprinted from one end of the garage to the other, and when he came to a stop, he realized this was the first time he had run. Theo dropped to his knees, and cried.

By early spring, just about everyone except Theo had declared victory. While walking again was big, he took that as a given, almost as a starting point, when most people around him saw it as the finish line. As every other goal in his recovery fell to his will, the goal to try snowboarding again loomed larger. For anyone who thinks of skiing or snowboarding as a nice vacation hobby to do once or twice a year or a few weekends out of the season, it is a little hard to believe that a simple hobby could be so important. For Theo, it was no hobby. From the day he first stepped on a snowboard in middle school, he worked relentlessly to become one of the best. Now, snowboarding had become central to his identity. With the end of the season fast approaching, he struggled to muster the courage to test his ability, fearful he would fail.

Our collective belief as a family was if he could get back on the snowboard, everything else would fall into place. If he could just snowboard, the minor annoyances left behind by his injury would become more manageable. His body was weaker.

His hand, "the claw" as he called it, barely worked. Anytime he yawned, his left arm inexplicably raised up, as though he were about to ask a question in school. His miracle toe, the first one he moved at St. Mary's, had become hypersensitive on the bottom. The toe was so sensitive that when he scraped it on something, a powerful rush of sensation flooded his entire body. He called it a "toe-gasm."

Buttoning a shirt, tying a shoe, or typing an email took him ten times longer than they did before his accident. He had to manage his gait consciously. If he forgot, he fell, especially going down steps. He had the bladder control of an eight-month-pregnant mother. All of this would be okay, or at least tolerable, we thought, if he could get back on the snowboard.

His optimism in reaching the goal drove him in his rehab. Even at Craig Hospital, his therapy sessions in the pool were oriented around this goal. His therapist would place a plank across a cylinder on the bottom of the pool, like a teeter-totter, to simulate the required balancing action of a snowboard. Theo would shift his weight front to back, balancing on the board, simulating the feel. He was thrilled to learn he could do this exercise, saying it was almost automatic, even easier than walking. The pool could not replicate a sun-washed, white-powder day on the back bowls of Vail mountain, which was what he craved.

We tried not to bring it up too much, but occasionally we would ask if he was thinking about trying to snowboard. He was, but he had not found the right time. One day, finally, in late March, he called to say he was going that next weekend and one or two of his friends would go with him. He was excited. We were thrilled and could hardly wait for the report.

Monday came and went, and there was no word. We had noticed a bit of a pattern forming, so that concerned us. He always tried to put his best face on when we spoke on the phone. When he called us proactively, which was rare, he was usually upbeat and conversational. When he was not in good spirits, we did not hear from him, he did not reply to our texts, and there was no activity on Facebook. The swings in this direction were becoming a little more frequent and were lasting longer.

I sent a text: "Hope it went well Sunday. Anxious to hear." No answer. Jorja sent a text: "We'd like to hear from you." No answer. I made an excuse to send an email, telling him about something that generally did not matter and finished with, "We are looking forward to hearing about last Sunday." By Thursday, we could not take any more, so we called. He was not in a good mood; he was even a little detached. His friends had been unable to go along, and he was too afraid to go alone, concerned he might hurt himself again, so he stayed home.

He was afraid to go snowboarding, something unimaginable before. Inside, though, he was waging an increasingly dark emotional war for his future. Jorja sensed it before I did, but the signs were there all along, in retrospect. She sensed it that day also and was very worried about the detached tone she heard in his voice.

He was so defeated. We talked for a while, encouraging him to try again. It was one of many phone calls where I felt so inadequately prepared. What he was experiencing was something I knew absolutely nothing about. He seemed to feel better after talking it through with us. I would give him suggestions, whatever came into my head, on how to think about and process the situation, that everything he was feeling was normal and expected. Jorja would tell him how deeply we loved him, how we were in his corner, and how we prayed for him constantly. I do not know. Somehow it all seemed to help. We suggested he call his good friend Conrad Ian and ask him to snowboard with him.

Jorja and I first met Conrad when we were in Vail to visit Theo one year, and Theo invited Conrad and his girlfriend Theresa to join us for dinner at a local restaurant. He goes by "Conrad Ian," but his real name is Ian Douglas McCarthy. The "Conrad" was a nickname he picked up in college, later dropped, and retuned to in his current job at The Boa System since there were already three other guys named Ian. He says, with a sort of sarcastic grin, "These days, I'm Conrad McCarthy, but I like to think that Conrad doesn't really need a last name . . . like Madonna or Bono or Morrissey."

Conrad is a tall, lanky kid, with his almost-black hair often pulled back in a short ponytail somewhere around the crown of his head, revealing pierced ears and a bony but handsome face. One look at him and any decent Italian mother would immediately try to feed him. I call him a kid, but he is in his early thirties. He is cool. He does not act cool; he just is. He is very particular about his clothes, but his style is to look like it is not important to him how he looks.

He will tie a scarf around his neck over a cotton jacket and pair it with blue jeans and sneakers in such a way that you might think, "He just picked up the closest things when he dressed today, but somehow he looks very cool. Very Colorado cool." He wears a permanent smile, which is hard to pull off and still seem genuine, but it is. His laid-back demeanor can fool, as well, because there is an intensity to him, which is a little hard to place. When you speak, he fixes his gaze on you and listens intensely, absorbs every word, and then pauses uncomfortably long, thinking first about what he will say before he answers.

We could tell how close the two were as they exchanged inside jokes and bantered over a wide range of common interests or the latest odd video clip they had seen streamed on

YouTube. Conrad is a thinker, like Theo. The two could spend hours cycling or hiking or snowboarding and sitting and talking through just about any subject. Theo spoke about him often and how much he appreciated Conrad's friendship.

Theo seemed to think reaching out to Conrad was a good idea, although he did not want to bother someone else with his problems. We were not sure Theo was going to follow up, so Jorja privately texted Conrad, asking him to reach out to Theo. Conrad called Theo to see how he was doing, and along the way, Theo mentioned he might be thinking about trying to snowboard. It was something they had talked about before, but it surprised Conrad when Theo abruptly told him on the phone, "I'm thinking about doing this; wanna come?" Conrad jumped on the offer, telling him, "I'm going with you. Let's go."

So they went on Tuesday, April 8, a bright, sunny, Chamber-of-Commerce sort of day. They began by just gliding down the beginner bunny slope, walking back to the top, and gliding down again. Theo had done it a thousand times before as an instructor with beginner students.

When that felt okay, they lined up to ride a chair lift, which is no small feat for a snowboarder. Skiers just keep both skies on during the ride. At the end of the ride, they hop off and glide down a gentle hill pushing with their poles to maintain momentum through flat spots. A snowboarder, though, does not use poles. One foot remains strapped to the board for the ride up, while the other foot is unlatched, so the snowboarder can push away from the lift with one foot, exactly the way you would to get a skateboard started. A much higher degree of coordination is required, especially since you are exiting a moving lift onto a slippery hill at the same time as two or three other skiers and boarders riding with you on the same chair.

Theo fell on the first try off the lift, causing a commotion as the operator stopped the lift and waited for Theo to move out of the way. It was the last time he would fall while navigating a lift, and Theo and Conrad spent the remainder of the afternoon carving side by side through the corduroy-groomed beginner slopes, Theo methodically reacquainting himself with the sensation and adapting to his new form.

"When he would fall, it was so dramatic," Conrad said. "His brain knew how to react to a situation, but his body couldn't tell him about it soon enough nor react to instructions quickly enough. So he fell in slow motion. He was also stiff and didn't have muscle tone when he would fall." He fell several times, but he got back up, as he always had done, and tried again. And each time he tried again, he was a little better.

"That day was a big deal for me," Conrad said. "Being involved in that moment, after he'd been told he would not walk again. It was a moment you could have faith that he could get back to what he was doing and go live a normal life. Just accepting the day for what it was, we had some good times and some awesome laughs."

Friend Brett Nevin also joined in for the day and snapped a picture of Theo on his snowboard, sliding gingerly down a cat-walk, a snow-covered service road used during ski season as a connector for skiers to cut across from one part of the mountain to another, usually on a gentle slope. Brett posted the picture on Facebook with the simple understated caption, "He's back." I showed the posting to Jorja, and our eyes filled with tears as we read the stream of comments. The last one was from Brett again. It said, "This was a good day."

15

"Revenge Is No Fun."

Theo's own perspective about his first day back on the snowboard was less than enthusiastic. "It was okay," he told us, "but it's not the same. I can't do anything I used to do." Jorja and I, deflated, encouraged him again, told him it was too early to say that and, in any case, he might have to think about snowboarding differently in the future, more as something to enjoy than something to conquer. When I relayed Theo's comment to Conrad, he explained to me, "What you have to understand is that Theo was one of the top two or three snowboarders on the mountain. And, even now, he is still one of the best snowboarders out there. He is just so hard on himself."

A couple of weeks after that first tenuous outing on the slope, though, Conrad and Theresa invited Theo to spend the day on the mountain again. With the nervous apprehension of the first outing in the past, Theo and Conrad spent the morning challenging each other to learn new moves or for Theo to relearn a trick he had lost. Teaching Theresa how to ride the half pipe in the afternoon, Theo realized what his mother, the teacher, had already told him. He had not lost the talent and the skill to explain and teach. The feeling was good. That evening, Conrad posted a picture of Theo suspended in midair on his snowboard, clearing a jump. I smiled. Jorja cringed.

The slopes closed, and spring began its turn toward summer. That is called "mud season" in the mountains. The skiers have gone home, the summer vacationers have not arrived yet, and the snowmelt is turning the valley into a big mud puddle. The locals take their vacations. Theo flew to Dallas on his first solo plane trip as a Mother's Day gift. He drove himself to the Denver airport, navigated security, and hoisted his bag into the overhead bin. He walked through the revolving door, out of security in Dallas, with a smile on his face, wearing the backpack we sent him for Christmas. He looked good—a little thin, but good. The dozens of business travelers rushing past in uniform, wearing blue blazers and washed jeans and dragging roller bags seemed oblivious to the magnitude of the occasion.

At the car, Jorja and I knew from experience not to offer help unless he explicitly asked for it. He pushed the strap of the backpack off his left shoulder with his right hand and swung the bag around to drop it into the trunk. Otto and Dietrich, who bark incessantly at every visitor, no matter how many times they have been there before, greeted him at the house with nothing but wagging tails. His visit was beautifully unremarkable. We had dinner at a couple of nice restaurants we thought he would enjoy, ate large amounts of Blue Bell ice cream, and visited about his work. He sat between us in church on Sunday. In the sermon text, the pastor said, "A woman who has a child immediately embarks upon a life of self-sacrifice for the sake of the child's well-being. She gives of herself in innumerable ways so that her child will be more."

We noticed one distinctive change in Theo during his visit. We noticed a softness, or humility, in his demeanor. A few tears were shed as we discussed where he was in his rehabilitation efforts, and his frustration boiled occasionally—for example, when he was late to meet us for dinner because he could not get his shirt ironed and buttoned. In the high moments, though, he had an appreciation for what had happened, knowing he had been inexplicably blessed in his healing. He thanked us for our support and told his mom how much he appreciated her. The edge of impetuous youth was gone. A compassionate man was emerging.

Jorja and I followed the same cycle every time we saw him. Over the weeks in between visits, we could settle into our routines. The visual images of his physical limitations were not there to remind us, and they faded over time. When we saw him, Jorja always went first, tucking her arms under his shoulders and bringing him close to give him a very, very long hug and tell him, "I have missed my boy." Then I gave him a firm, manly sort of bear hug, long enough to analyze in my mind how it compared to last time, but not too long.

Each time, we were reintroduced to the fact he still struggled every day. The first moments were always unsettling as we watched him navigate the kitchen, bend to scratch the dog behind its ear, or pick up a coffee mug. We studied every movement, hoping he did not notice, looking for subtle signs of improvement. A day or so would pass before I could begin to focus on something else. By the end of the visit, we were acclimated, but saying goodbye just restarted the agonizing cycle. It never got easier. With each goodbye, some pieces of our hearts were ripped away. Jorja was especially affected, far more painfully than if the accident had just happened to her instead.

After Theo's visit, Jorja and I went on a long-planned trip to Scotland with close friends. Outside of that trip, I was traveling heavily in a new role with my company, and Jorja was becoming deeply involved in moving her parents from her hometown of Sedalia, Missouri, to an assisted living facility in Kansas City, Missouri. Her mom was in the middle to late stages of Alzheimer's, and her dad was too frail to take care of the house, the two acres of land, and Jorja's mom.

As Jorja was checking on her parents, Mae's wedding plans were also heating up. She would be married in Dallas, but she was working in Plymouth, Massachusetts, so Jorja also was bearing the bulk of the work in planning the wedding. Mae came to Dallas on the Fourth of July weekend on a whirlwind tour to decide on food, get fitted for the dress, and attend a shower.

All the signs coming from Vail were positive. It appeared Theo was enjoying the summer and was opening a new future. He had purchased a circa 1970 vintage Rollei 35mm camera at an antique store in Leadville and was taking black-and-white photos and learning to develop them himself. He was also getting more into music, especially house music, and was producing mixes using loaner equipment he would then post on SoundCloud.

One morning in late July, Theo strapped on his backpack, heavy with a tent and other camping gear, and set out alone for Gore Lake, a twelve-mile round-trip hike through rugged terrain, climbing 2,700 feet. He posted on Facebook, "So the hike was unrelentingly challenging with my pack fulla tent etc., but the views were worth it. Can't wait to see how my early morning rollei35 shots come out." But the chasm between how he looked to others and whom he saw in the mirror months before in the therapy gym was growing.

He was still getting physically stronger, he was working, and he was returning to some of the things he loved and developing some new interests. Inside, though, he was churning. He continued to be frustrated, feeling that many of his friends were no longer communicating with him. The worst frustration would happen when someone would say, "You must be so thankful. At least, you can walk," or, "At least, you're right-handed." He obsessed about whether he had done the right thing in splitting with Coni.

Theo called home every couple of weeks or so, which was a blessing and a curse. Rightly or wrongly, our own temperament hung on those calls. If he was in a good mood, Jorja and I were, too. If he was not, we worried after we hung up. On his worst days, he was lonely, and he didn't see a path forward in his life. If we felt he waited too long to call home, we worried about that, too. We would reach out to him, which was usually unsatisfying. If he had wanted to talk, he would have called us. Occasionally, he would call and ask for help. When an issue was very important to him, he still came to us. He usually ended the call in what seemed to be a better mood, appreciative of advice we saw as inadequate. Parsing his sparse words for signs of hope or despair in his complex, highly fortified psyche from a thousand miles away was exhausting.

In Vail, Dan Miller had a ringside seat throughout the summer. He patiently supervised Theo at work, figuring out what position he could fill until he was able to do more and taking the brunt of Theo's emotional highs and lows as his manager. Working the front drive at the Ritz was replaced by answering phones in a windowless room or organizing ski lockers in the basement. "Seeing him fight through every day, with guests who think they have big problems," Dan said, "made it tough for me to balance the professional side with the ridiculous perspective that Theo was managing through. He has this ability to suppress his own situation and be so tough on himself. He breaks it down to every single interaction he has with a guest."

When Theo did occasionally work the front drive to help in peak hours, he could not lift the heavy suitcases or move as fast to retrieve a car. Self-conscious that he was only holding the rest of the group back, cutting into their shared tips, he retreated. The "Blast Brothers" contest Theo had instituted among the valets in the spring before his accident was gone. The contest was a parody of one of the regular hotel guests who was a workout fanatic and often explained some aspect of his workout with the term *blast*, like "I just blasted through those push-ups!" Theo installed a pull-up bar and various weights in the bell house, and the idea was that each time a member of the drive team passed through the bell house, that person would need first to perform their maximum number of push-ups or bench presses before moving on.

A trip back to Vail in late July to celebrate Theo's twenty-sixth birthday offered Jorja and me a chance to see Theo firsthand, and that left us confident he was beginning to turn a corner. One morning, he took us on a gorgeous two-and-a half-mile hike, rising steeply through aspen and conifer groves to a ridge, and then to Lake Whitney, nestled into a quiet valley surrounded by dense forest. We were alone at the lake, and the still water reflected a perfect image of Whitney Peak rising from the north shore.

With the one-year anniversary of his accident looming just over the horizon, we were optimistic. Theo was still raising the bar. In July, when he returned to Craig for a six-month evaluation, he began to seriously discuss the option of taking a Botox treatment again with Dr. Berliner. The benefits were not obvious, but some patients found relief. It would potentially weaken muscles which were overpowering his left arm and hand so that the weak muscles could have a chance to gain strength. Still operating in the "try everything" zone, Theo decided it was worth a shot. A reluctant Dr. Berliner acquiesced because he knew Theo was never going to be satisfied unless he had exhausted every potential option. They agreed to schedule the treatment.

The process dragged, but the hospital finally scheduled him in on his birthday, August 9. He was excited to get on with it, hoping it would return acceleration to his recovery that had been lagging. When he arrived for the appointment, he learned he was there only to complete a battery of tests and the actual treatment would be later. In the whole scheme of his recovery, a few weeks was not the end of the world, but he had so prepared himself for this day, the next big step in becoming normal. He was devastated to have to wait again.

Theo called me from the parking garage outside Craig Hospital after being sent home to wait. He was on the third floor of the garage in the corner, where no one could see him. Speaking with me through tears, he was peering over the wall of the garage to the ground three stories below, wondering if maybe he should just throw himself off and be finished with it. He was extremely frustrated, upset that the hospital had not made clear the purpose of this visit. He had anticipated it for weeks. His physical improvement had stagnated, and he was in the first real plateau. He had taken the day off from work for the two-hour drive to Denver from Vail and was imagining how the Botox treatment would make a huge difference after today. He wanted something to happen, but now, the treatment still needed to be scheduled for some unknown future date. In this moment, to him, jumping over that short wall was a plausible solution.

On the other end of the call, I had no idea that this was what he was seriously considering. Of course, he told me he was frustrated, he still did not feel he was pulling his weight at work, he could not ride his road bike as he used to, and he felt he was a burden to his friends. He was in between two hells. At Craig Hospital, he was a superstar. He no longer belonged there, and he did not want to be there. In Vail, he was the weakest and slowest in a culture where everyone was fit and enjoying the outdoors.

I do not know how I would have reacted had I been there to see him looking over that wall. Had he told me at the time, I am sure I would have been on the next flight out of Dallas. What would he have done if I did not answer the phone? I cannot think about it. What matters is that he did not do it. Instead, he gathered his composure, got in his car, and drove back to Vail to wait and work.

He called a week later to let us know he had taken a short trip on his road bike with a few friends. He enjoyed the time with friends but continued to be frustrated by how he struggled with his power and with gripping the handle bars and switching gears. We used the call to broach the idea of his visiting the site of his accident on the anniversary date, but we cautioned him not to do it alone. He thought that asking for someone to accompany him would be an imposition, but when he floated the idea to Dan, Scott, and Eric, they jumped at the opportunity. Everyone, apparently, had some unfinished business on that mountain.

The four were brought together by the mountains, all living examples of the often-repeated adage "we came for the winters and stayed for the summers." What kept them together was mutual respect, a common interest in helping people, and a shared passion for the outdoors. What bound them together now and for good was a shared tragedy and the need to answer the question, "Why me?" Dan, Eric, and Scott did not run off the trail and suffer the physical injury, but they were also survivors, deeply impacted by the experience. Why did this happen to them? Were they somehow responsible? What should they do about it? These unvoiced questions were already percolating when Dan called Jorja the night of September 17. The questions were written on their faces when Jorja and I walked into the St. Mary's ICU and met them for the first time.

The group left on September 16 and drove to Crested Butte, just as they had done a year earlier, but this time without the mountain bikes. The sense of excitement and adventure a year earlier was now replaced with introspection and anxiousness. They had pizza in the restaurant they were planning to eat at the night after their ride on Doctor Park. The next morning, about the same time they would have left to ride it the year before, the guys piled into a car and left for the mountain and the dirt parking lot that had doubled as a makeshift rescue headquarters. Few words were spoken.

Eric, the person in charge of loss prevention at the Ritz and the eldest of three kids in his family, carried a heavy burden of accountability. He was the only one who had ridden the trail before and was sure he should have stayed with the pack, ensuring they knew about every surprising turn. If he had done that, he thought, the whole thing never would have happened. Dan felt responsible, too. He was the most senior among the three at work and had been the one to invite Theo on the trip. Scott, the bell captain, was easily the most athletic in the group.

Maybe he pushed too hard. A believer in karma, he was stung by a bee just about the time Theo crashed. Although he was much farther down the trail, he knew something was wrong.

The mood was far from "light and playful," as had been described a year earlier. Hiking up the hill from the opposite end, they had difficulty gauging how near they were to the accident site. They knew only approximately how far to go based on recollections of hiking down the trail after they had left Theo in the hands of the paramedics. Theo, of course, had no recollection of the path.

Sensing they might be nearing the site, the three guys hung back a few yards, giving Theo some space. Rounding a slow bend, slightly uphill, they spotted the accident location, or at least what they thought was it. They were not certain because a year of growth and decay had passed. Trees had grown and fallen, paths had shifted, and last year, what the path looked like in the moment had been the least of their concerns.

When Scott Everhart pointed him to the tree they thought it must have been, Theo lay down on his back beneath it, with his head near the trunk and his feet toward the path, and looked up into the sky. He knew it was right. The opening to heaven was right there, a blue patch of sky surrounded by golden aspen leaves fluttering in the breeze, right where he had left it. He cried a little and walked around. He surveyed the curve of the trail, the rollers, imagined the place he must have lost control, and the trajectory from there to the tree. He approached the tree again, took out a knife he had brought on the trip, and carved a large "TK" into the bark on the back side, away from the trail. Near the bottom, he carved the words "REVENGE IS NO FUN." He put the knife in his backpack, unzipped his pants, and urinated on the base of the tree. One could almost hear the words echo through the forest: "Fuck this shit." Then he turned his back and walked away. Theo's Facebook posting on September 17 read:

I don't like doing personal updates much, but I would like to list all the things I was able to do today that I was told I would not and should not have ever been able to do again as of a year ago:

Woke up, sat up in bed, walked to the sink, brushed my teeth with no help using a normal toothbrush, & combed my hair using a normal comb.

Got in and out of a car driving to breakfast. Then I ate a normal breakfast using normal utcnsils.

Tied my shoes, put sunscreen on, and started on a hike.

Walked up a steep & sandy downhill trail 3 miles.

Carved my initials into a tree with no help then urinated on the same tree with no help.

Walked down a steep & sandy downhill trail 3 miles.

Sprinted to the bathroom, took a dump by myself with no devices or medicine, cleaned myself up, stood up off the camp toilet, and jogged back to the car.

Rode in a car for three hours without having to worry about shifting my weight. At one point, I was even able to feel my right buttock go numb due to my wallet.

Got home, used a normal key to let myself in, showered (able to clean almost every square inch of my body by myself), got dressed, and I'm on my way to meet friends for a beverage in the village.

When I'm having a hard day where I feel like I am
light-years away from being 'recovered,' I try to remember these things. More importantly, I try to remember
the people who made me who I am. The resiliency in
my character is due to you. So, in simple terms, I owe
you a "Thank you."

Thank you.

By the first anniversary, I was aware of only one person
still wearing the "I'm a Theo" purple bracelet. We had lived
the year between heaven and hell, as Theo describes it. Healing
has exceeded any rational measure of hope we had in the first
days. The therapists are inspired; the doctors are speechless by
what they see. Theo can walk, run, and ride a bike, and he
plans to teach snowboarding in the winter. There is a strong
lesson, which probably should have been learned many years
ago: no matter how much you hover, no matter how many
baby monitors, car seats, hand sanitizers, Louis Vitton purses,
helmets, and houses in gated neighborhoods you buy, no matter
how many background checks, parent/teacher meetings, recommended pediatricians, ballet lessons, or top-ten universities,
children will at some point get hurt, and you won't be able to
fix it. Only they will be able to fix it, but they will have help.

Aspen trees are said to be the world's largest living organism.
They do not exist alone, but as a grove, all connected through a
single root system. So it was for us. A community of friends, family,
and caregivers brought us to this one-year anniversary, connected
by a root system of faith at some level. One of those deepest roots,
Theo's mother, was the one still wearing the bracelet. She bore the
pain on the very first day and would run with him to the very last
day, looking for some way to help make every day better.

16

Theo Dances

Even as he acknowledged the immense progress he had made in the past year, by the time Theo typed "Thank you" into his Facebook post, he was already moving the goal posts on his way to normal.

The Botox treatment was finally scheduled for September 18, the day after the one-year anniversary of his accident. He was elated afterward as he gave Jorja and me a full description about how it was done. It was exciting to him how they zeroed in on the hot spots in his muscle system and inserted the needle in precise locations up and down his left arm. He was sure something would happen.

Something did happen. For about a week, the Botox relaxed him. He could feel the drug dampening the spasms and relaxing his taut muscles, returning some balance. Then things began to deteriorate. He felt like a wet noodle by the time Mae's wedding came along in mid-October and began to realize he was suffering the effects of an unlikely risk he had discussed with Dr. B. The Botox toxin was seeping into his entire body, not just the arm he was trying to help.

We did not see it when we collected him at the airport in Dallas for the wedding. Jorja remarked he seemed a bit thinner, a little frailer. I disagreed, blaming it on loose-fitting clothing. I was, frankly, too preoccupied being father of the bride to notice. I had joked about the upcoming wedding for months, but the truth was that I was afraid I was totally losing my daughter this time, not like when she went away to college. I thought that was tough! This time, though, I was being replaced, and it was the cause of a big party. Still reeling from flashbacks of the day Jorja pulled her wedding dress out of the box and let Mae, about sixteen at the time, try it on and parade in front of me without warning, I could not bear even to watch Mae's dress-fitting. As the big day approached, I spent hours sifting through and then posting old pictures of Mae on Facebook with nostalgic captions about "letting go" and how I was never warned about this before having children.

I had two essential tasks to get right at the wedding. First, I needed to walk Mae down the aisle without breaking down into a crying, drooling old man, and second, I had to get through the father-of-the-bride reception toast without breaking down into a crying, drooling old man. I made it down the hundred-foot aisle, barely. The ceremony had been traditional and simple, the bride and groom beaming at each other through the entire affair. The church setting was elegant. The music was perfect. The pastor's homily was exceptional.

When my pastor dedicates a baby in worship, he counsels the parents to raise the child "in the precincts of the temple" and encourages the congregation to be active participants in the child's formative years. Then he finishes by reminding the parents, "God does not promise an easy life, but a good life. This child does not belong to you. She is a gift from God and with you only for a time." He repeated the same words in his homily at Mae's ceremony. These words were no longer just liturgical tradition but a tangible reality to us as parents of Mae and Theo.

Theo stood to read the Scripture from a small, black vinyl folder. Almost no wedding guest outside our family knew the folder dripped with historical significance. My father had used it throughout his career when officiating weddings and funerals. He had used the folder in our wedding, too, thirty-one years earlier, but he accidently dropped it in the men's room urinal minutes before our ceremony began. He smoothed his crinkled notes as he turned from page to page, and my two groomsmen brothers looked on with smirking grins. That folder not only represented a story of my beginning with Jorja. It held the legacy of my father, his ideology, and the generations who formed him.

My father's ancestors were a group of hard-working Mennonite German farmers who brought their way of life to Molotschna, Russia, in the eighteenth century at the invitation of Catherine the Great, then immigrated to the United States in 1874, bringing along Russian red-wheat seed to grow America's bread basket. Goodness, discipline, and perseverance were hallmark traits of the Alexanderwohl Village they established in central Kansas. Those same three traits of Jakob Krause and Anna Kroeker; of their son, Abraham Krause, and his wife, Maria Janz; and of their son, Adolf Krause, and his wife Maria Thiessen—my father's parents—were also stuffed into that two-dollar vinyl folder.

The black folder had also appeared on the table next to Dad's picture in a packed church sanctuary for his memorial service on a cold February Saturday in 1995. The path my father took from his boyhood home in Gotebo, Oklahoma, born in the teeth of the Great Depression as the oldest son of a poor wheat farmer, to the places where he had played some pivotal role in each of these people's lives was unlikely. Drafted into the Navy for World War II, he used the GI bill to become the first and only child in his family to attend college. There, he met my mother, Mae Adeline Pitney, a doe-eyed Missouri girl with a beautiful soprano voice and a passion to be a missionary. Dad wanted to be a preacher. By the time they retired more than four decades later, they had begun dozens of churches and impacted thousands of people, one by one, from Bavaria's Black Forest to Missouri's Ozark Mountains.

The over two hundred guests filling the sanctuary for Mae and Dale's wedding had, in some way, participated in their formations and represented the participation of hundreds, maybe thousands more, who had come before them. As people streamed into the reception tent after the ceremony, I thought, "How wonderful, how appropriate we are sharing this event with people who have meant so much to us, especially during the past year."

I will remember that evening to my last breath. A cold front pushed through Dallas the night before, bringing a torrential rainstorm that had the tent company scrambling all night. The storm left behind clean air and a crisp fall afternoon. Equal parts of relief, celebration, and anticipation filtered through the warm glow of the wedding tent lighting. I could not have imagined a more magnificent setting for a celebration of marriage, of family, and of life.

One friend had counseled me that I needed to be sure to take the time to fully enjoy the moment because it would pass quickly. At times, I felt as though I were stepping outside myself, looking over the whole spectacle from a distance, unable to grasp the idea that all these people in this moment had chosen to celebrate our good fortune and Mae and Dale's prospective future.

The reception tent was filled with warm conversation and laughter, and the DJ, the photo booth, the signature cocktails, and the candy jars were all in their places. A buffet of food stretched the length of the tent. All the people in the room understood the magnitude of the occasion, and their optimism permeated the mood. They shared a unanimous belief that no matter what might happen from here, the future was bright. When that many people invested their attention, their talent, their optimism, and their hopes all on the dreams of my family, my fear of losing *Mae* was pushed aside by an overwhelming sense of joy.

I made it most of the way through the toast, but I worried I would not get through reading an important excerpt of a Helen Keller passage from her book, *The Story of My Life*, a favorite of Jorja's mother. She was already at an advanced stage in her battle with Alzheimer's, and Jorja found the excerpt in her mother's things as she was preparing to move her and Jorja's dad into an assisted living facility. To me, these words perfectly captured our sentiment on this occasion and how we felt about the people in that room, but to read it aloud brought me dangerously close to my threshold of emotional control.

In a last-minute decision, I asked Theo to step up and read it, which he did. "There are red letter days in our lives, when we meet people who thrill us like a fine poem." For a split second, I worried I had made a big mistake by having him hold a microphone in one hand and a piece of paper in the other in front of a bunch of people. He marshalled on, "People whose handshake is brimful of unspoken sympathy and whose sweet rich natures impart to our eager, impatient spirits a wonderful restfulness, which in its essence is divine. The complexities, irritations, and worries that have absorbed us pass like unpleasant dreams, and we wake to see with new eyes and hear with new ears the beauty and harmony of God's real world. In a word, while such friends are near, we feel that all is well."

I trained my clouded eyes on Mae and Dale, raising my champagne glass to deliver the final words of my wedding toast: "To Mae and Dale, may the world around you be obese with love." I caught Jorja's eye, only for a brief but intense glance. I had stolen these words from Chris Jones, a close friend of Theo's who had written the phrase on a get-well card when Theo was recovering in the ICU, and I looked away just the instant before losing my composure. We both knew more than ever what that could mean.

The sound of two hundred champagne glasses chinking together kicked off the best party I ever attended. Jorja and I were facing uncharted territory with adult children and the idea that we no longer had any direct responsibility for the success of either of them. Jorja, who retired from teaching music the spring before Theo's accident, would be shifting her attention toward her aging parents. For now, she beamed as she watched the new couple's first dance and meandered from table to table, chatting with guests, reaping the reward of six months of meticulous planning.

The question, "What about me?" had rattled around in my head like an elusive loose screw in the dashboard of my car for thirty years. A long career of steady promotions took me to the C-suite of a large corporation, which always felt more like hard work than mission or purpose, more like I was a frog in a boiling pot. I was not so sure I had honored my heritage or made a difference in people's lives. At some point, I would need to decide if the time had come for something radically different. For now, I reveled in the moment as I looked out at those who had done so much for my family.

I was particularly proud of the specialty cocktails I had invented for the bride and the groom. The bride's cocktail was essentially a Bellini and was called "Thank you, rider" in deference to Mae's equestrian passion. In a jumping competition, if the rider goes off course too far, the rider hears these dreaded words from the judge, indicating the rider has been disqualified. The groom is a paramedic, and his bourbon-and-honey-based cocktail was called "Put me on a stretcher."

Mae's wedding day marked a transitional moment for all of us, and we were going to have to learn to create a new kind of normal. It would be one where each one of us was risking leaving behind what we knew best to pursue a future we could not predict. Mae was crossing a threshold from a familiar world, not dismissing her past but combining it with Dale's to start a new world, launching into the risky business of building a new existence. Mae, the namesake of her grandmother, also understood the importance of the black folder, having chosen her grandfather's birth date as her wedding day.

What would have escaped an uninformed visitor was the seemingly ordinary but truly absurd fact that Mae's brother Theo walked calmly down the aisle as a groomsman, stood later in the service to read the Scripture from a black folder that my father had used throughout his career as a minister, and finally brought the house down during the wedding party dance competition with his rendition of "the sexy dance," much to the embarrassment of his bridesmaid partner, the groom's twin sister. Only the DJ and the service staff were surprised when the crowd roared its approval while Theo danced.

17

Theo Searching for Theo

Wurge hen Theo brought the house down with his rendition of "the sexy dance," he was putting on a show, giving people the version of him they had expected. That he had been told just one year earlier he would never walk seemed ridiculous, like a sick practical joke. Now he was the prankster. Hidden behind the façade of the miraculous healing he believed everyone needed to cheer lurked a darkening spirit of resignation. Theo was at a threshold of his own. He would finally decide whether he wanted to expand the narrative for the next generation.

The closer he came to normal, the way he used to be, the more focused Theo became on what he could not do. Getting back on the snowboard did not feel "normal" at all, leading him to conclude the idyllic sense of normalcy he doggedly pursued throughout his recovery might never happen. Carving the first tracks on a fresh ski slope for him was like a painter painting on a fresh canvas. "Telling me I should find a way to enjoy snowboarding again," he told me, "would be like telling Picasso he should find a way to enjoy painting again after having his right hand cut off." While hanging such importance on snowboarding may seem overly dramatic to someone who just skis or snowboards as a hobby on family vacations, for Theo snowboarding was definitional. His passion had left him, and he was losing his way.

Snowboarding was only the flag-bearer for a much more radical problem. From the time he left home, moving to Denver, then to the mountains, Theo had built his adult identity and his ecosystem of relationships around physical achievement in an active, fitness-conscious, outdoor culture. Snowboarding, road biking, hiking, camping, weightlifting, whatever it was, he wanted to be the best among the best. He once had the ability to do it. This was now gone. In his view, everything that most defined him in the world had been taken away.

Theo told no one except his close friend and hotel roommate for the weekend, Joe Cardinal, what was really happening because of the Botox injections. From the moment he stepped off the plane, he determined not to do anything to sour the mood of Mae's wedding. Theo had relearned a hundred mundane daily tasks he could have performed without a second thought before the accident, but the routine he had worked so hard to rebuild was already falling apart as the Botox invaded his dexterity.

I could tell he was in a foul mood when he arrived thirty minutes late for the photography session before the ceremony, but he was tight-lipped about the cause. "Nothing," he said curtly. "There was a mix up in communication about how I would get there." Unable to do them for himself, he finally enlisted Joe to tie his shoes, to button his buttons, and to hook his bow tie around his neck. "I asked too much of myself," Theo much later conceded. "I got frustrated." But Joe, who likes to call himself Theo's "PLP," or Platonic Life Partner, would not let Theo "fall into a depressed pity party" as he hustled him out the door to catch up to the wedding party, where Theo smiled on command in every photo. Above all his frustrations, Mae was what mattered most to him then.

One week after Mae's wedding, Theo went to Iceland with Phillip Cherry, a friend he has known since elementary school. He originally booked the trip for himself and Coni when he was still in Craig Hospital, but after they split in the spring, he asked Phillip to step in. Phillip quickly accepted the invitation, asking, "Who turns down a trip with their best friend to one of the coolest places on the planet?"

Theo realized he was in even more serious trouble during the trip. The Botox had permeated his entire body. His balance faltered. His hard-won dexterity retreated further. One day, near Lake Jokulsarlon, on the southeast coast, he fumbled with a tripod set up for his camera until a puff of a stiff wind blew it over. The camera plopped into the water, ruining the film. He fumed inside. "We were in this perfect 'Martian-like' landscape, and I wasn't all there," Theo told me. "I felt like someone with clinical depression must feel like in a tropical paradise like St. Lucia. They are in this most perfect place, and they just can't seem to be happy."

As the trip progressed, a deep sadness seeped in beneath the Botox, but he welcomed it. He had complained before, even before he was injured, that he sometimes felt no strong emotions, positive or negative. This emotion of sadness was at least strong—so strong that it was memorable and powerful. "You can't synthesize deep sadness," he explained. "Anything that powerful and overwhelming is kind of addictive." He knew instinctively, though, that he was on his way to a bottom. From there, it would be up or out.

Phillip could not see how much the Botox was taking its toll. Theo masked his condition well, and the only frame of reference Phillip had for Theo's physical condition came from a visit to Vail in January. The two had spoken by phone a few times, but nearly a year had passed since Phillip had actually seen Theo. Phillip could, of course, sometimes see Theo's frustration at his difficulty in buttoning a shirt or tying a shoe. "Theo might throw a sock or some other soft object across the room," he said. "But that was about it." Phillip would offer to help, but Theo usually rebuffed him unless timeliness overrode the importance of pride. From Phillip's perspective, it was humbling and emotional, almost a sacred privilege, to be allowed to tie the shoes or to button the coat of the person he considered to be his lifelong best friend. He later told me by phone, "It would be hard to take a more meaningful trip than the one we took to Iceland in 2014."

By the time Theo returned from the trip, most of the gains in strength he had made since moving home in January were lost to the Botox treatment. Intellectually, he knew the loss was temporary and the drug would be out of his system soon, but muscles atrophy much more quickly in a person who lives with reduced neurological function from a spinal injury. If he wanted to get back to where he was before the treatment, it would take hard work—hard work he had already done once.

Everything was wrong. The days were shorter. The sky was gray. It was cold. Theo could barely button his shirt to go to work at the Ritz, and he could not do what he wanted once he got there. He was a burden on the rest of the team. Snow was falling, but he did not want to be on his snowboard, even if he could do so. It was no longer fun. Dressing and tying boot laces took forever. He could not snowboard the way he used to, anyway. Friends were scarce. They were too busy with the tourist season starting. He had had little luck in the relationship department since the split with Coni.

Theo was no stranger to the use of marijuana now and then, having attended college in Colorado. He began using it more frequently after his accident, especially at night, because it calmed his spasms before bed. His usage increased as it became a crutch to insulate himself from his emotions. He was also "using alcohol" as he put it, referring to that winter as his "clinical trial period of drug use." It worked as a duller and kept him from facing himself and his future. He kept up appearances with friends and at work, but Theo was miserable. Something needed to change.

Theo is an analytic person, and one of his favorite subjects to analyze is himself. Craig Hospital provided counseling services during his rehab, and Jorja and I convinced him to see a therapist earlier in the year. Theo went one time. He said the therapist gave him some helpful hints and reading suggestions, but "there was nothing he said that I had not already processed two or three layers deeper." That was true, I am sure, but this therapy was the one area I thought he did not give enough of a chance to help him heal.

One day in late October, he concluded he could decide what he wanted his future to be, or if he wanted one at all, only with a clear head. He was self-aware enough to know why he was "overmedicating" himself, so he stopped everything, cold turkey. He went fully sober for twenty-five days, just to see what would happen. "When I stopped," he said, "I really had to face it. I had to figure out what I wanted to do next. I thought very hard about what was important and what needed to continue to be important. At that moment, what was important was living the way I did before the accident." There were two very viable paths, one of which seemed very straightforward and rational. For him, ignoring the impact on anyone else, the right path was to commit suicide.

"No matter what happened," he reasoned, "death would produce a radical change." Whether there was no life after death, whether he came back as a cat or a sumo wrestler, whether he went to heaven, or even if he did not die from the suicide attempt, it would nonetheless produce a radical change. That would be better than this current life. That thinking may sound absurd, given the extraordinary recovery he had experienced. How could he not be thankful for the healing and excited about the future? According to the experts, this battle can be much more difficult for people who have had an incomplete spinal injury than people who know their fate from almost the first day. People with a complete injury have a determined outcome, and they can get on with how they will live. With an incomplete injury, one never knows where the end is. Theo was always guessing as to whether he was going to get better or if today was as good as it would get. Living with that unknown prevented him from putting his past behind him. Not only had the Botox treatment he was so optimistic about let him down, this state of living with an unattainable past had also become intolerable.

We did not hear from him for at least a couple of weeks. As we had done before, we texted to ask how he was doing. No answer. I called, but it went to voicemail. I asked him to call back. He did not. Finally, he called Jorja late in the afternoon on November 19, as he occasionally would do if he was feeling especially lonely or depressed. This was one of those times. He was not in a good mood. He spoke about how nothing was right. He no longer liked to snowboard, he could not pull his weight at work, it did not seem he would ever find someone to share his life, and he just did not feel there was any good reason to keep going. What alarmed Jorja the most was the tone of his conversation. He was detached, unemotional. He spoke without inflection, as though he were reading from an encyclopedia or a dictionary. Jorja reminded him that he had so much for which to be thankful, that he had friends who would help him, and, most of all, that we loved him.

When Jorja hung up the phone, she was afraid for his safety and called me. I was staying at the airport hotel in Frankfurt, Germany, on my way home from a European business trip, when she reached me. She told me I needed to call Theo right away. She was worried he was about to do something serious. We agreed that in the meantime, she should reach out to Meg Cahill and ask her to check on Theo. She was as close as any friend he had, and we knew she would follow up.

Perpetually youthful, Meg is a young woman destined to be carded at bars and restaurants for many years to come. Her azure eyes and a persistent wide grin melt the coldest hearts. She has a natural beauty, with slightly wind-kissed cheeks and long, flowing brunette hair. Meg looks like she belongs in Colorado, at home in the outdoors, often dressed as though she is about to go skiing or hiking or has just returned.

Meg met Theo through his Craigslist posting for a roommate. She was traveling through Europe the summer of 2011, working on an organic farm in Denmark when she answered the posting. After a few introductory emails and a Skype call, she asked him to hold her place until she moved to Vail in November. The two became friends quickly, but their styles were so different they could barely tolerate each other after a while. He was too critical and inflexible; she did not listen and was irresponsible. After a big blow-up argument and a subsequent cooling off, they apologized to each other and sat down to work it out. They became close friends from that day, and it formed the basis for how Meg would help him through some of the most difficult emotional moments of his life.

A nervous pit swelled in my stomach as I picked Theo's name from the "favorites" list on my cell phone. I was relieved when he answered, "Hey, Dad." Like so many times before, I had no plan for what to say. "Hey, Theo," I started. "What's going on? Mom said you were a little down." He repeated essentially the same story Jorja had passed along to me, although he was a little more present now. Jorja's encouragement seemed to have registered somewhere.

Electing to try to convince him that what he was feeling was normal, I reminded him that his doctors at Craig Hospital had told him this time was coming for him. I reminded him that we had said we would be with him, no matter what it took, that his close friends also were with him, and that we all felt everything he felt. If I could, I would take his place. I told him to promise me he would not do anything to hurt himself, and he did. I was not so sure. "I love you too, Dad. Bye" were the last words I heard before hanging up.

By now it was 2:00 a.m. in my tiny, bland room buried in a hotel in the middle of an airport a million miles from anyone at the top of my favorites list. With no chance I could sleep, I called George Mason, who had been there in our home that first morning we were about to leave for Grand Junction. I recounted to him my conversation with Theo. George assured me that no matter what Theo decided to do, we had done what we could. We were paying attention, we reached out, we said the right things. The rest would be up to Theo. I was not seeking George's affirmation, but it was important to hear.

More important, he suggested Jorja and I might need to step back some. "It is his pain, and you shouldn't try to take it from him," he counseled. "Parents always want to shield their kids from pain. It's natural for you to say you would take his place, but even if you could, that would rob him of what he might learn and who he might become because of it. Pain is a gift that invites us to come to terms with loss. The key is to focus on him, not his pain. So, instead of asking how his pain feels, you might ask him how he feels about his pain."

George suggested that we might be feeding his anxiety with ours. "Backing off doesn't mean caring less but caring differently," he continued. "By tending to your own anxiety instead of his, you automatically reduce it and stop the feedback loop that you can all get caught in." Theo may have sensed we were hanging on his every sentence, and he did not want that to keep happening. That could help, but it just as easily could deepen his own anxiety.

Jorja, meanwhile, had successfully reached Meg: "Do you remember you told me if there was ever anything you could do to help, just to let you know? I need your help now." Seared in Meg's memory was the shocking sight of Theo lying in the St. Mary's ICU and their first tearful exchange. "I just need you to be the friend you've always been," Theo told her. She replied, "I love you, and we are going to figure this out."

Meg was a frequent visitor during Theo's recovery but moved out of the apartment to take an au pair job in the spring. She had been traveling quite a bit and had not seen or spoken with Theo for some time. She agreed to reach out and let Jorja know what she found. Meg posted a message to Theo's timeline on Facebook: "Hi. That old flip phone died on me so I lost your number. I was waiting for you to text me but you never did . . . gawd. Drama I hateeee it. Anyway, I got a newer version flip phone. −AND I also won a gift certificate to el Sabor. This has our name on it. Much love to you, text me so I have your digits."

He responded and agreed to dinner. "I came over and saw that he could not even tie his shoe," Meg remembered. When she asked him about it, he shrugged, "It is what it is." He refused to discuss it at first, but Meg, a consummate optimist, pressed. As they visited, or the more she talked, she coaxed him to talk through what he was experiencing. He confessed he had convinced himself the early progress he made would continue. Now he was angry it had almost stopped. He was also lonely. "It's pointless to be here," he told her. "There is no purpose for me, no purpose for my life. I couldn't protect a female. I'm not a strong man anymore, and I could not even protect someone I love."

Meg took Theo to a nearby sports bar for a beer, unsure it was a good idea, given both his physical and mental state. Then they went to cash in on the El Sabor gift certificate, where he began to let loose a little. She could see his mood lighten as the effect of good food and the familiarity of a friendship seeped into his eyes. After dropping Theo back at his apartment that evening, she called Jorja with an update and said she would reach out to him in some way every day for two weeks. Each day, Meg sent him a text message or left a surprise gift on his doorstep. "I just tried to keep him knowing I am here," she said.

A week after the dinner with Theo, Meg met Kevin Pearce, the pro snowboarder whose documentary film had introduced Theo to Craig Hospital, at an event in Vail. She sat down with Pearce and told him Theo's story. He was amazed, and Meg asked him, "But could you reach out to him? He is in a dark place right now." She gave him Theo's email address, and he agreed to write. Excited she had made the connection, she waited days for Theo to say something. Unable to wait any longer, she asked Theo if he got an email from Kevin. "Oh, yeah, I got it." That was it. Expecting him to be cheered up by the gesture, or at least to elicit a smile from him, she was deflated, uncertain if she had made a difference.

18

A Coalition of Friends

Theo later thanked Meg for her gesture, but during those critical November days, a nice email from Kevin Pearce was no more than spam, a distraction from the heady question of survival. While most people around him were counting blessings, deciding which traditional delicacies to prepare for the family Thanksgiving dinner, he was deciding between life and death.

His thought process was analytic, at least from his perspective, arriving at two alternative tenets: one, to die was better than to live with his limitations, and two, to live, even with limitation, was better than to die. The first choice was best for him, he thought. All the arguments he developed over the months about his lost physical ability and the realization he would never return to his complete self were stacked on death's side. Even his colleagues at work would be better off. He was holding them back.

Other than colleagues, though, the second tenet, for life over death, was better for everyone else. In the limit, he simply could not tolerate the thought of putting his friends, his family, and especially his mother through the pain, notwithstanding his December 25 journal entry almost one year earlier to the contrary. Meg had reminded him only days before how he had scolded her for making an irresponsible choice leading to her snowmobiling accident. "If anything worse had happened," he told her through his own tears, "it would have hurt a lot of people. Me. Your family." Committing suicide would be the ultimate selfish act, in his mind. His decision was to live.

A consequence of such a decision, he knew, was that he needed to plan for the rest of his life. Theo came to Dallas the second weekend of December to attend a high school friend's wedding. I picked him up from the airport, while Jorja stayed home to finish cooking some of his favorite holiday treats. During the drive home, he was so full of stories and ideas I had to ask him to stop until we got home so his mom could hear them, too. I live in constant fear of not remembering to pass along to Jorja a story one of our kids has told me. He had exceeded my storage capacity.

When we walked into the house, the sweet scent of fresh zwieback, my grandmother's German bread, hung in the air. Jorja had not seen Theo since the night he called her in such deep despair. "Oh, it's soooo good to have my boy home!" she gasped, barely able to push the words past her heart as she rounded the corner out of the kitchen and reached around his waist. He dropped his bag, wrapped his arms around her, and pulled her in close. "It's good to be home, Mom," he whispered. His tone was warm and tender, the way it sounds when someone speaks through a smile, with no hint of the detached resignation she had heard only a month before. The optimistic young Teddy, who had assured her, "It'll be okay, Mom," before he disappeared into the kindergarten building, was home. The scared young man, Theo, who had needed a physical therapist to place his limp arms around his mother in the ICU and who had then said, "I love you, too, Momma," was home. The deeply lost Theo who had written, "I wish I could crush her spirit," in his journal one Christmas ago was also home. Theo was profoundly changed. So was home, but he was home.

The Botox had taken its toll but had retreated. He was certainly thinner, having lost substantial muscle mass through the ordeal. As he stretched his arms around his mom, several new tattoos came into view on his left forearm. An Icelandic compass, an Airblaster pterodactyl—his favorite snowboard brand because he says, "They like fun and dorking around"—and a flying saucer because if he could go anywhere or do anything, he would go to space. When I asked why they were all inked into his embattled left arm, he quipped, "I call it my 'fun arm' now." Theo was on his way to regaining what he had lost. Most important, he was thinking about the future and setting goals, like restarting the pursuit of his top snowboard instructor certification. Theo was only in town for a couple of days, but as he disappeared behind the security checkpoint on his way back to Denver, Jorja and I knew he had reached a turning point. He was clearly embarking on a new quest, looking toward a new definition of himself, of who he was to become.

Theo, unable to come home because of his holiday work schedule, called home on Christmas Day. Still pondering choices about the future, he used us as a sounding board for his ideas. Maybe he would take on a bigger role at the Ritz, or maybe he would open a restaurant. He wanted to spend more time working with his music. Theo has a unique knack for remembering lyrics, even if he has heard a song only once, and he relishes identifying inner themes in the work of other artists or the clever use of a phrase or rhythm.

He decided to return to teaching snowboard lessons, discovering he could experience as much enjoyment from watching a kid "get it" as he could from doing it himself. He thought, as his friend and fellow Craig Hospital patient Jon Atwater had done, he might buy some property and later build a house on it. As the year closed and a new one began, Theo had essentially done again what we had watched him do so many times at St. Mary's and at Craig Hospital. After tough and frustrating days, he awoke the next morning, collected his thoughts, and willed himself back to work, unwilling to concede his goal. He was also different, but a good kind of different.

As the parade of people inserting themselves to help Theo expanded to include those who had helped him after the dramatic rescue and his extraordinary recovery and rehabilitation in the hospital, the theme of people helping people at just the right time deepened again. Not only were strangers showing up at the right moment with unique capabilities to fix things I could not fix and without my asking. Not only did most of those people radically change course, finding their passion or vocation after a dramatic, life-changing event. Not only were most of them influenced in their chosen path, the one which intersected Theo's life, by a strong parent or mentor. Those who helped Theo were also influenced by his response to adversity. The influence of people coming into any life is a two-way street, especially when those people are friends, rather than complete strangers.

Theo's friends did not just make a dramatic entrance in a flash of time; they were there from the beginning and stayed past the end. The friendships he cultivated were his most valuable resources in the long run. The friends who invested in him—who knew him before he was injured and stayed with him after he was injured—were also deeply changed by his experience. Sometimes Theo saw himself as alone, but he was never alone. Theo's friends grieved, healed, and changed with him.

Meg had been present throughout the ordeal. As was the case with all the others, she brought a life experience perfectly suited to the situation. Born into adversity as a premature baby and barely escaping with her life after an automobile accident at age seventeen, she knew as much as anyone what Theo was experiencing. She went to college at SUNY "because everyone went there" and the price was right. She set out to travel the world immediately after her graduation. Then she spent a year-and-a-half working with children in San Francisco and several months camping and backpacking through Australia, and she helped rebuild a home outside of Stockholm. She loves food, kids, teaching, and the mountains. She summed up her life approach like this: "If you have a head on your shoulders and are willing to put yourself out there and integrate into the culture, people will help."

She was the first to visit Theo in the ICU outside of his family and his three mountain biking friends. She regularly visited him at Craig. She was there the day we dropped him off in Vail, and she was a lifeline for what may well have been the most life-threatening time in his recovery. What she did for Theo was no less than those who were involved in his rescue on the first day or any of the other people who had helped him so far. I believe she talked him off the ledge on November 19, 2014, and just may have saved his life.

When Meg speaks of how the experience of Theo's ordeal affected her, she says, "It has changed me. It's the most humbling thing I've ever been a part of. Life is so precious. It's so important to appreciate what you have and who you are with. Somewhere he had angels looking over him. But he had to decide to do the work. It inspired me to want to make progress all the time in my life at anything I do. He helped me as a teacher. I learned from Theo to listen to learn."

Dan Miller had known Theo longer than anyone, since the first season Theo was in Vail, parking cars for Dan at the Marriott. Dan was born in Marietta, Ohio, to a farmer and a school teacher from a long line of school teachers. "Marietta farmers grow four major crops," he says. "Beef, hay, corn, and football players." That last one got Dan a scholarship to college, but his love of travel landed him at Muskingum College to study international business, a summer job in Anchorage, Alaska, and a first job driving a bus during the winter season in Avon, Colorado, just down the road from Vail.

Their symbiotic recovery was best described the first day Dan saw Theo's toes move in the St. Mary's ICU. "To see him move his toes, and to be looking out over the Grand Mesa and how beautiful it was," he reflected. "We were at the age where we have been through some things. That was a reminder that there was hope. In that setting, we are still where we want to be in our place in the world."

Theo sees the change in Dan, even if he is reluctant to attribute it to his own influence. "He has grown up so much," Theo said. "I would run my mouth, and he would listen to me and take it in. He's kind of like a big brother." Dan was more pointed about it when he said, "Theo keeps me in check, and I keep him in check, and it is love and mutual respect. I love he can articulate things better than me. Even when I disagree, he has a reason why he thinks that way, and he is unwavering in his commitment to that thought. I remember the day he pulled me aside when I didn't handle a guest situation very well. He looked me in the eye and said 'Dan, I think you could have handled that better.' I was his manager, but I thanked him and said, 'You're right.'"

Scott Everhart may have assigned special significance to the bee sting in part because his father was a beekeeper. Raised in a town of 117 people called Artesian, South Dakota, Scott describes himself as "the only kid in my class of twenty who did not know how to drive a tractor." His dad was also a volunteer firefighter, and his mom was president of the School Nutrition Association. After a false start at South Dakota State, Scott transferred to Northland College because "they had a lake and a forest" and a major in outdoor education with a focus on teaching people with disabilities. An internship to the Breckenridge Outdoor Education Center brought him to Colorado, where he discovered helping disabled people succeed was the most rewarding thing he had ever experienced. "They are the happiest people you'll ever meet out in the snow, doing something they never thought possible," he said.

Coincidentally, Scott admires a similar quality he sees in his friend Theo. "Theo's one of the happiest guys you'll meet," he said. "When he is there, it is brighter, and the accident didn't change that." He also works to expand out of his comfort zone because of Theo's influence. "He and I listen to different music," Scott said diplomatically. "When I was driving Theo's car to Grand Junction, I went through most of that iPod before I found a song I liked. I put it on repeat." He admires Theo's eclectic style and sense of humor, but Theo says, "Scott is where I get my monk-like tendencies. I was attracted to how stoic he is."

Eric Sjoreen still struggles to make sense of Theo's accident. Eric loved the outdoors just as much as the rest of the guys, but he was a big-town, big-school kid, moving from Chicago to Pittsburgh in the eighth grade, then attending Penn State to get a degree in its School for Recreational/Park and Tourism Management. "I think about the people that have stood behind me, and who I look up to. He is one of them," Eric Sjoreen told me. "It makes me happy that nothing slows him down. It will be close to my heart for the rest of my life."

The common themes in the stories of all these friends are easy to spot: teachers or children of teachers, lovers of travel and the outdoors, an acute sense of awareness and responsibility for people in need. The theme extends to many of his closest friends, including Conrad Ian, Phillip Cherry, and others. Like-minded people coalesce. Each person was following his or her own path, usually plotted initially by a parent. Later, without thinking too much about the implications, each one made choices which led them to a common place.

Where they came from, the fundamental values instilled in them by their parents, and the choices they made themselves as adults collectively brought them to a moment in the mountains. In an extraordinary sense, who they are now as individuals has changed in large part through the influence of one another, through their differences, and through their choices to risk investment in a friendship.

The three guys—Dan Miller, Scott Everhart, and Eric Sjoreen—saw the situation differently, at least in the beginning. All harbored some form of guilt for not taking better care of their friend, playing over and over the actions they should have taken to change the outcome. Jorja and I could see their questions in their eyes, but they can also attest that Theo, Jorja, and I see the situation otherwise. If they were not listening when we said they were not guilty, they can see that they are blameless with these words. We do not blame them or anyone else. It was an unfortunate, unlikely accident, with a lightning-rare outcome no one could have anticipated. Given the opportunity, they would make the same choices again. They would move to the mountains, become friends, and decide to spend a beautiful fall weekend riding together. Every time. We do not hold our pain against them. We hold their pain with them.

One thing is certain. Every time they hear the ominous thump of helicopter blades and see a flash of the helicopter's orange underbelly passing overhead, they are transported, for a moment, back to the memory of a beautiful fall day and an aspen tree next to a stream at the base of a ravine. That day happened a long time ago, and they are now different, closer to who they will ultimately become.

19

From the Beach

For Jorja and me, meeting the friends surrounding Theo in his life after he left home for college was enlightening and a huge relief. We knew what life we wanted for our kids. We did not know, and it was not our place to know, everything about everything in their lives, but at the least we wanted to know whether he had established a good network of friends. As a result of his accident, we had the opportunity to witness a parade of impressive friends. Reflected in their eyes, we also found a glimpse of the man Theo was becoming.

The optimistic Teddy we knew as a child had not disappeared. Ted, the often procrastinating, brooding high school senior, who was more than ready to leave home, was also still there. We knew him to be happy and funny at times, serious and too hard on himself at other times, with occasional flashes of anger. He was a perfectionist when he cared about something, but he knew how to do just enough to fulfill an obligation he deemed pointless.

From the very first day in the hospital in Grand Junction, Jorja and I were surprised to discover a previously unknown Theo. When we saw him seize meticulous control of his own care even while he was heavily medicated, when we saw him memorizing the names of his caregivers out of respect, and when we saw him focus every ounce of energy on his rehabilitation, we swelled with new pride. To his friends, Theo was just being Theo.

Theo is an amalgamation of his heritage, of his mother and father, and of the choices he has made and the experience he has gained along the way. Almost two years later, he is an older spirit, softer, more appreciative of what he has, more sensitive to the feelings of others. He is almost too conscious of the impact of his own actions on others, if such a consciousness is possible. By his own admission, he had been myopic, too narrowly fixated on his personal physical conditioning and his expertise on the snowboard. Suddenly, a range of new values and goals is emerging as the mountain loosens its grip on his soul. How these changes are resolved in Theo's future is an unwritten story. He must write those pages.

The mandate is not just for him. The course of every person who was touched by his accident has changed. Farid Tabaian, the first person to find him on the mountain, said, "It has changed the reason and the way I ride." Farid has never been back to his favorite trail, Doctor Park. Irene Rüesch, who held Theo's head in her hands for hours, said, "It's in my life, and it will never leave me." Scott Everhart will "never listen to a helicopter the same way," and Eric Sjoreen has "a flashback every time I sit on a bike."

Mae, Jorja, and I are also changed. Mae was in the middle of her own set of life-changing events at the time. She had graduated from college, was interviewing for her first job, and was getting married. She often could not be physically present through her brother's recovery. She could not sit by his bed, as Maggie Ireland had done for her brother. Theo's accident was life-altering, nonetheless. Mae is more resolute in her own faith, and the experience has brought her closer to Theo. Her foundation has been rocked by the idea that someone with Theo's active lifestyle could have everything taken away in an instant. When she does something that requires dexterity in her hands, she thinks about Theo and whether he would be able to do the task. Their relationship has evolved from the mutual indifference of young siblings to mutual respect as adults.

Jorja is less carefree in life, in a sense having lost her innocence about the future. She is more measured and a little less optimistic. Saying goodbye to Mae or Theo after a call or a visit is even more difficult for her than before his accident. In the back of her mind, she wonders if the goodbye could be the last. Yet she is intensely proud of how she perceives that Theo has grown. "Not that a mother would ever choose this cause and effect," she stresses. "I still wish it had happened to me, instead, but this whole thing so matured Theo and opened his eyes to the 'obese love' around him. He inspires me to get up and move because of what he can do. When he goes hiking or running or camping, it makes me want to get up and do something, too. If he can do it, why can't I?"

The impact of Theo's accident even traces to those who had no direct involvement in it. Most probably do not even know Theo's name. I sent Rob Weisbaum, the Care Flite paramedic, an email on the anniversary of Theo's accident with an update on how well Theo's recovery had gone. He answered, "I thought of you and Theo today because I am teaching our EMT class right now, and tonight's topic is spinal cord injuries. Theo's story will forever stay with me. I shared this story tonight and showed my students this email. They were inspired by Theo's story as I expressed why I love my job so much."

With the immediacy of Theo's battle easing, I was just beginning to unravel the impact of the experience for me as a father, the impact on my career, and the impact on the long-held, previously unchallenged tenets of my theology. The seams of my own identity, the way I was raised in a Christian home, patched together with my education in the natural laws of physics, had never been so severely tested for strength.

When Jorja and I decided to take a February weekend getaway about as far from any mountains as we could be, I had ample time to think. Sitting under an umbrella all day on the beach in Cancun, Mexico, I cycled through a series of naps, turning questions over in my mind and reading *Christians as the Romans Saw Them* by Robert Louis Wilken, a great story about the perspective of secular Romans as the Christian faith found its identity in the early years of the movement. Jorja was lying in the full blaze of the sun, reading Anne Lamott's *Small Victories*. I do not much like to swim in the ocean, to lie under the baking sun, or to get sand in my shoes walking down the beach, but being seated under an umbrella with nothing but the sound of the crashing surf—accompanied by a gin and tonic and a Cuban cigar—has a clarifying effect.

With my toes firmly dug into the cool sand, I thought about how many of the people who helped Theo found their vocations or passions, connecting into their deepest sense of identity. The people who effected Theo's recovery were able to do so only because they had found and followed their individual passion or purpose in life and stepped out to play their role in a critical moment as their lives intersected his. For some, it was an exceptional experience; for others, it was simply the nature of their work.

Most of these people found their vocations through some type of loss, a personal tragedy, or a door closed in the path they always had in mind for themselves. Irene could not follow her first dream in child care, Rob Weisbaum's parachute jump nearly killed him, Dr. Berliner lost his eye to cancer, and Maggie nearly lost her brother in the Columbine shooting. All of us, including me, are still in some stage of "finding Theo," in the sense of understanding our gifts, in understanding our place in the world.

Wendell Berry, poet, writer, environmentalist, and farmer, says, "The old and honorable idea of 'vocation' is simply that we each are called, by God, or by our gifts, or by our preference, to a kind of good work for which we are particularly fitted." As Theo came into his dawn at the end of 2014, I was also, for the first time, seeing a new dawn of my own. Never considering my job as my vocation in the sense of Wendell Berry's definition, I decided I would tell the story of what I had seen. I also decided I needed to plot a course away from my corporate job and toward something new. Whether the two would be connected somehow, I did not know.

I do know this: losing and finding are two sides of a coin. In an instant, on a mountain in Colorado, Theo's life changed forever, and my life changed forever. A half-degree, one way or the other, and Theo misses the tree. A millimeter more compression, and his spinal artery is severed, and he bleeds to death on the mountain. In a split second, on a bridge in Houston in

1991, the course of my future could have been altered in an unfathomable way. It was not, or maybe it was.

I looked up from reading to watch several twenty-something parasail operators working feverishly to unsnarl a tourist from a massive, brightly striped parasail with a huge "Dos XX" splayed across the back. The boat pilot revved the engines into reverse to reduce the tension of the tow cable as the rest of the crew worked to prevent the lines from tangling and to unsnap the harness from their helpless customer.

Fixing things, I also discovered, is a team sport. When I walked into that ICU room the first day, looked Theo in the eyes, and essentially told myself, "We're going to fix this," I didn't realize at that point that others had already started "to fix this" without my asking. Dr. Clifford recognized he was a mere facilitator of healing, as did Dr. Berliner and Dr. Hsu. Thankfully, Erik Forsythe, a world expert in mountain-rescue operations, had enough sense to realize he needed the help of the Western Mountain Rescue Team to get Theo off the mountain. The entire medical infrastructure—from Gunnison to Grand Junction to Denver—worked together with one common purpose: to try to fix Theo.

In Cancun, we were into our second day, and my purpose was less ambitious. I just wanted to remember the name of the waiter who greeted us every morning for breakfast at our beachfront hotel and the name of the bartender who brought my gin and tonic in the afternoon. I learned from my son that names matter a lot. Names matter because of what they represent. George Mason introduced the idea the very first morning after Theo's accident when he said in his prayer, "Help us to remember that who we are is not defined by what we cannot do." Now I have seen what he meant.

Jorja chose her name on the day she was adopted as a five-year-old. It was a symbol of her discovery of her own worth. Mae was named after her grandmother, Mae Adeline, a fact she has always cherished. Her grandmother went by "Adeline," so she chose to be called "Mae" to establish her own distinct identity.

When we were first abruptly directed by our son to use "Theo," the name meant absolutely nothing to me. I would say, "Theo," when I remembered, but I meant "Ted." I rarely make the mistake of reverting to "Ted" today, and if I do, it usually happens when I am talking about something that happened long ago. When I speak of him in the present, who he is today after everything that's happened, I cannot imagine using any name other than "Theo."

Being close to the sheer magnitude of mountains or the massive power of the ocean always has the same impact on me. The two spectacles represent the extremes of the world, yet they are only miniscule artifacts of the universe. I am always reminded how small I am. By our last afternoon in Cancun, maybe the cumulative effect of the massive waves bombarding my senses had broken through. Jorja sat calmly next to me, or so it seemed. She was soaking in the final rays of sun, which I know to have been created tens of thousands of years ago as gamma rays and traveled about eight minutes and ninety-three million miles to warm her face.

What I did not know was how a creator of something that big could be so involved in the smallest details of the tapestry of individuals appearing, as if on cue, ideally suited to meet my son's deep need in that moment. Some of those who helped Theo have also reflected on their belief systems since the accident. Farid Tabaian believes in some "higher power." Irene Rüesch agrees, saying, "You can call it God." She identifies more with Hinduism. Christine resonates with the principles of Buddhist life but regards her encounter with Theo as a simple, random event.

Dr. Clifford, an unapologetic Christian who lives that understanding daily, is blunt: "Miracles happen all the time. You just have to be paying attention." Rob Weisbaum agrees, saying, "I've had several incidents in my career where I really call them a miracle. This was one of them." Dan Miller joins Dr. Clifford and Rob Weisbaum, but he is honest about the conflict: "For me it is witnessing a miracle. And I don't necessarily believe in miracles."

Jorja is forceful and clear on the matter: "I am unwavering in my belief that God bent His ear to the prayers of His people and to our son's deep need. Now I know that, even at the bottom of the riverbed, we are not alone. God meets us there and sits with us."

I have learned more than I wanted to know about the inherent power of the body to reconnect and repair itself. While the tissue in the spinal column has no regenerative power of itself, the whole nervous system has the capability essentially to rewire itself. Stressed but undamaged nerves can shut down for a while and then wake up when it is safe for them to do so. The brain can relearn alternate paths through the nervous system to its intended target.

The words of John Polkinghorne, a particle physicist turned Anglican priest, suddenly made practical sense. In his book *Quarks, Chaos, & Christianity*, Polkinghorne says, "The feeling of wonder at the beautiful structure of the physical universe, which is so fundamental an experience for the scientist and is the reward for all the weary labor involved in scientific research, is a recognition of the mind of the Creator."

What if our world, like the human body, is a connected organism where people, whether they believe it or not, and whether they know it or not, are working independently toward a common purpose? If people work with determination to find their passions, or vocations, they will encounter moments for which they unknowingly have been preparing. Most people will encounter many such moments in a lifetime, as my father or any one of the medical professionals in this book did. If they see those moments and engage in them, something important happens.

The building block of the complex system I witnessed as people came to Theo's aid was created by the simple process of finding one's way in life. In this sense, a miracle is much, much bigger than one God intervening in one life at one moment to make my son walk again. The miracle is how the creator of everything is intrinsically involved at every moment with every life, for all time. The natural world was made to work that way. The dogma of original sin in Christianity, that we are all born evil, is incomplete. People are inherently good and seek to do something good in the world. The scientific principle entropy, of a world in decay, is also incomplete. The world is in a constant state of creation, as ashes fertilize new life and people find their way.

This idea is plausible only if it works for everyone, including Tim Bowers, who broke his neck in a deer-hunting accident and chose to decline life support six weeks after Theo's accident. The news reporting about Tim was preoccupied with the question of whether it was appropriate to decline life support. On the night after his death, his new wife, Abbey, who was three months pregnant with their son, sat alone with his body in his room, crying, and asked herself, "What am I supposed to do now?" She says she never felt so completely alone. Then rescuers began to arrive.

Her sister invited her for Christmas so she would not be alone. Her best friend, Amanda, knew just what to say at the right time. Her mother took care of her oldest son while she mourned. Her dad, she says, is her hero. He tells her, "I will take care of you. You shouldn't worry about anything." She has met a companion named Nate who, she says, " is one of the best things to ever happen to me." Nate treats her youngest son, Jasper, the new life she carried forward as Tim slipped into death, as his own.

Theo walked again. Tim Bowers did not. Does this mean there was a miracle for one but not the other? Possibly. I do not know. The miracle I witnessed was the one Chris Jones described in his card to Theo. "The world around you is obese with love."

All that is required, if we want to be part of such a world, is to find our "Theo," to find our way to our gift to the world, to our God, to our good work to which we are each particularly fitted. For Theo, his search began with his own relentless determination to find his way and to reject the limitations of the scenario he was given.

Just two months before he died, I was standing with Dad in the garage after we had cleaned up from a small project. He wore his coveralls while resting his elbow on the broom handle and looked out past the driveway and the front lawn. "Sometimes, I wonder. When I get to heaven and I am standing before Saint Peter and the Lord, will I feel like I have done enough with my life, or if I have done all I could do?"

What I have found is that this question is unanswerable in the context of a world where every instant in time is made possible by everyone who has gone before me, everyone who helps me, and a creator who makes it all work.

The wind on our Cancun beach was up, and the red flags were flying. Brilliant turquoise waves swelled to a deep blue, then violently crashed into seething foam as they raced up the beach, only to retreat quickly and rendezvous for another attack. Jorja and I linked hands, left the protection of the umbrella and the comfort of our chaise lounges, and headed toward the sea.

A submerged sandbar provided a sort of shelf, which both instigated the destruction of these unsuspecting waves and, at the same time, provided some footing for us to brace against the force and resist the undertow. "The ocean can do as it pleases," I think, "and we are powerless to control it." We paused on the sandbar, facing the open sea.

After a few thoughtful moments spent peering intently beyond the horizon, Jorja peeled the faded, purple bracelet from her wrist and threw it with all her might. We watched as it plopped into the sea, drifted, and slowly disappeared into the dark. A wave crashed through us. We stood together in silence and cried.

In the darkest hours, our most horrifying fear was that we would lose Theo. Part of Theo was lost. There is no avoiding this hard truth—not by us, and certainly not by him. But much has been found. I recalled what Frederick Buechner said: "What's lost is nothing to what's found, and all the death that ever was, set next to life, would scarcely fill a cup." This is not what I believed on September 17, 2013. I believe it today. Well, most days.

Epilogue
Theo Krause

My dad says I have always chosen the difficult over the safe, relishing the challenge, but when a mountain biking accident left me with a broken neck and a spinal cord injury, my perspective of a challenge shifted to surviving, recovering, and adapting to a new "normal." Through fortuitous rescue by strangers, emergency surgery by gifted physicians, relentless rehab guides, and the love and support of my family and friends, I have had the opportunity to learn that joy can come from suffering and that empathy leads to happiness. These lessons did not come easily.

I am not an optimist. In fact, I would categorize myself as a pessimist or, better yet, a realist. My hyper-rational brain allows me to digest problems, ideas, and solutions. I can get so involved with observation about situations that I never take action. I'm thankful I didn't do that when I got hurt. I did just the opposite. I stopped thinking too much and decided on a singular goal which would lead my recovery: I was going to prove them all wrong and walk out of the hospital. I was going to snowboard again and cook again and bike again and run again and dance again and sing again and love again and make love again. I was going to do everything again.

Daily, I had to fight through the daunting examples of how I was, in fact, not going to do any of those things again. I was going to end up in a wheelchair, confined to my own prison. I was going to need help going to the bathroom and eating and sleeping and brushing my teeth and taking a shower and putting on my clothes and getting back to work. I was going to be alone forever. I was going to miss out on the endorphin rush that comes from just being active. I was going to be a cripple.

I wish I could have convinced myself that physical ability could operate independently from the potential for happiness. I'm still working through that one. I still get frustrated with certain physical inabilities. I dislike that my arm twitches, that my hand is jammed up, and that I cannot work and type as fast as others. I worry that my potential jobs are now limited because of my conditions. I feel powerless because I don't have the potential to be a top runner or professional chef or racecar driver or fireman or snowboarder or banker or plumber or housekeeper or waiter or whatever, but I have been given the chance to do something more than existing with a feeding tube and a respirator. I am alive, I am well, I can remain mentally strong, and I can remain physically strong. I can still set goals. I can choose not to be overwhelmed. I can still cook and clean and be independent and love and like and flirt and manage myself and make goals and pursue aspirations and make new friends. I have had a rebirth and can choose to be worth a damn. So that's what I choose.

I don't often think about my condition from an all-encompassing perspective. It comes out most frequently as a simple desire to use my hand normally. I would love not to have to think about extending my wrist or my fingers or grabbing something or releasing that same object. I want to be able to do pushups and pullups and every other normal body manipulation. I'm still scared to go on group runs or bikes or workouts for fear of abnormal bodily functions ruining the experience for others. I don't want to have to explain myself, and I feel obliged to, nearly always. This is a problem I need to get over.

I went out with an old acquaintance from high school recently, and my injury did not come up. We met at 6:30 in the evening and parted at 11:15. That is a long time to talk with someone and catch up on life but never bring up the single most life-changing event that has ever happened to me. What if others don't look at it the way I do? Yes, my accident changed me and my goals and aspirations but not how these people know me. My friend and I had a great meetup. I realized I am able to hold a conversation with someone who is smarter and more informed than I. That motivated me to want to learn more instead of focusing on my inabilities so often.

Somehow, when we go through life-threatening injuries, we are expected to become wise and share our insights with others. There is a Tibetan saying that wisdom is like rainwater; both gather in low places. I have gained a lot of wisdom from this low place. I didn't ask for it, but sometimes you end up being the most thankful for the nicely gifted pair of socks you would not have wanted when you were younger. It is a stretch to say that breaking one's neck is a positive event; however, it is not a stretch to say that it has given me a reason to use more of my capabilities and develop more resiliency. I am wise enough to know I am not wise, but I am also wise enough to realize how to use the wisdom I do have.

I discovered that, for me, wisdom begins with "I can." When I slipped on the ice and fell, I realized that I will not shatter. As I did at my sister's wedding, sometimes I like to go dancing—just because I can. I prefer to walk home from my job instead of taking the bus—because I can. I prefer to take the stairs instead of the elevator whenever possible—because I can.

As a result, I am excited about the prospect of a new direction in my life. I am leaving the mountains of Colorado, the sites of my greatest joys and my greatest despair, to start a new job in Washington, D.C. I take with me the marvelous memories of biking, snowboarding, and teaching others to enjoy the mountains, as well as the wisdom earned in the low places of pain. Perhaps my dad was right. I relish the challenges of my future—because I can.

Not to make loss beautiful,
But to make loss the place
Where beauty starts. Where
The heart understands
For the first time
The nature of its journey.

—Gregory Orr, *Concerning the Book
that is the Body of the Beloved*

Acknowledgments

To the professionals of Gunnison Valley Health Hospital, Saint Mary's Hospital, Craig Hospital, the Western Mountain Rescue Team, and Tristate CareFlight: Our family will never forget that your quick response, your teamwork, your compassion, and your dedication to your field made the difference.

To St. Mary's Hospital Rose Hill Hospitality House: You provided Jorja and me a quiet place to rest, regain our composure, and gather strength for the next day.

To my friends and colleagues at Alcatel-Lucent and AT&T: You worried with me, covered for me, and encouraged me to write this story. You still ask, "So, how's your son doing?" or "When is the book going to be finished?"

To Theo's many friends and colleagues: You're overwhelming support in the early days of Theo's recovery was a constant source of encouragement as Theo faced his new future. We are convinced your continued vigilance throughout his journey is the reason he is still here. Thank you for paying attention.

To my editor, Dr. Janet Harris: Your wise and steady, patient guidance helped a beginner carve a story from a jumbled mass of words. The next time should be easier, I hope.

To my publicist, Cindy Birne: Thank you for believing in my story, for your advice and counsel in navigating the wacky world of publishing, for tolerating my obsessions about every word and phrase in subtitles, bios, and catalog descriptions. The energy you are putting into the success of this book could power a thousand missions to Mars.

To the people of Wilshire Baptist Church: You were helping us many years before we knew we needed help. You taught our children what they would need to know, provided a sanctuary, and took on our tragedy as if it was your own.

To my friends Michael Capps, Steve Brookshire, and Dr. George Mason: You listened patiently as I obsessed over every idea, iteration, and revision. You encouraged me when I needed encouragement. Often times, you didn't say anything, which was perfect.

To my elder siblings, Vickie, Steven, and Philip: You worried, prayed, cried, encouraged, celebrated, corrected grammar, suggested words, and whatever else you thought was needed. I may never figure out when to use "lay" versus "lie," but I will always be grateful to have travelled my life in your wake.

Timothy Krause spent thirty years in high technology, ultimately serving as chief marketing officer of one of the world's largest telecommunications products suppliers. Today, he provides business strategy and marketing advice as an independent consultant, and he is a popular motivational speaker. He is a director of the World Affairs Council of Dallas-Fort Worth. He received a BA in physics from William Jewell College and he holds an MBA in business management from the University of Dallas. Timothy met his wife Jorja, a music education major, during a college choir tour. Together they have raised two children, lived and worked abroad in Paris, France, and currently reside in Dallas, Texas.

Theo Krause is a concierge for The Ritz-Carlton, where he has been nominated five times and twice received their top service award, the Five Star Award. Also a snowboard instructor for Vail Resorts, he passed the Professional Ski Instructors of America and the American Association of Snowboard Instructors Level 3 Certification in 2015, two years after his accident. Theo holds a BA in international business with a minor in economics and a BS in French from the University of Denver. He recently moved to Washington, D.C. together with his adopted cat, Oliver.

To learn more or schedule a speaking event, visit:
www.timothykrausebooks.com